Samina ...

May 89

Malcolm X Toronto, ONT

THE LAST SPEECHES

MAGNETIC HILL

MAGNETIC
HILL

Facing page: Speaking at Corn Hill Methodist Church in Rochester, New York, February 16, 1965. *(Photo: Gannett Rochester Newspapers / Peter Hickey)*

MalcolmX
THE LAST SPEECHES

Edited by Bruce Perry

PATHFINDER
New York London Montreal Sydney

ISBN 0-87348-543-2 paper; ISBN 0-87348-544-0 cloth
Library of Congress Catalog Card No. 89-61591
Manufactured in the United States of America

First edition, 1989
Fifth printing, November 1992

Cover and book design by Toni Gorton.

Cover photo by John Launois/Black Star.
The publisher thanks Robert Haggins, who has provided photos,
some of which appear for the first time in this book.

Pathfinder
410 West Street, New York, NY 10014, U.S.A.
Fax: (212) 727-0150

Pathfinder distributors around the world:
Australia (and Asia and the Pacific):
  Pathfinder, 19 Terry St., Surry Hills, Sydney, N.S.W. 2010
Britain (and Europe, Africa except South Africa, and Middle East):
  Pathfinder, 47 The Cut, London, SE1 8LL
Canada:
  Pathfinder, 6566, boul. St-Laurent, Montreal, Quebec, H2S 3C6
Iceland:
  Pathfinder, Klapparstíg 26, 2d floor, 121 Reykjavík
New Zealand:
  Pathfinder, La Gonda Arcade, 203 Karangahape Road, Auckland
  Postal address: P.O. Box 8730, Auckland
Sweden:
  Pathfinder, Vikingagatan 10, S-113 42, Stockholm
United States (and Caribbean, Latin America, and South Africa):
  Pathfinder, 410 West Street, New York, NY 10014

CONTENTS

Acknowledgments

F OR THEIR assistance in helping to make this book possible, the publisher and editor are indebted to C. Eric Lincoln, Minnie Clayton, Merlin Duncan, Richard Nesmith, Terry Denbow, Richard Hafner, and Nelson Lavergne. Special thanks are due to Abdullah Abdur-Razzaq and to Mark Brown, who checked several typed transcripts against the tape recordings from which they were made.

Introduction
by Bruce Perry

FINDING James 67X Shabazz, who supplied the tape recordings of most of the speeches that appear in this book, was not easy. None of his former colleagues seemed to know where he was. His name was not listed in any New York City phone book, despite the fact he reportedly lived in Brooklyn. Hard as I tried, I couldn't ascertain his whereabouts from any of the usual sources. Mr. Shabazz—now Abdullah Abdur-Razzaq— had dropped out of sight.

Then, around 1974, someone told me I might be able to locate him through the St. John's Recreational Center in Brooklyn. I drove there one Sunday and asked a friendly supervisor named Al Welch if anyone knew Mr. Abdur-Razzaq. Mr. Welch called over Bilal Abdullah and Abdul Malik. One of them—it's been so long, I forget which one—said he knew the man I was seeking. I wrote my name, address, and phone number on a scrap of paper, and asked him to forward them to Mr. Abdur-Razzaq. When I telephoned two or three weeks later, I learned that one of my would-be conduits had been killed in a confrontation with some of Elijah Muhammad's followers. The other, understandably, declined further involvement.

So I was back to square one. I stayed there three more years. Then I learned that Abdullah's wife had established a school for young children. When I finally located it in mid-1977, I was ecstatic, for Abdullah had been one of Malcolm X's chief aides.

My joy turned to despair when Abdullah's wife told me he had moved to South America and carved a farm out of virgin rain forest. The despair became depression when I learned that the nearest telephone facilities were several days' journey from his Guyana farm.

So I wrote. Abdullah's first letter, dated March 13, 1978, arrived eighteen days later. (Other letters took far longer.) He explained that his farm is about twenty-five miles from what used to be Jonestown. The nearest river port or airport—the only efficient method of travel in rural Guyana is by water or air—is thirty-one miles away. The roads are unpaved; even sturdy trucks cannot negotiate the enormous craters in them. So the only way to reach Abdullah's farm is to walk or hitch a bone-breaking ride on the tractor-drawn mail wagon that makes the trek about once a week.

For the better part of a year, Abdullah and I corresponded. I explained that I was writing a biography of Malcolm, and that I had interviewed his mother, four brothers, two sisters, most of his childhood neighbors and playmates, the majority of his former teachers, and scores of his ex-classmates, ex–prison mates, and former political associates. Finally, Abdullah agreed to meet me on the Caribbean island of Grenada, where Malcolm's mother had been raised. I was hoping to make contact with her Grenadian relatives. Eventually, I did. But that's another story.

During the spring of 1979—just a few weeks after Maurice Bishop's New Jewel Movement overthrew Eric Gairy's oppressive regime—Abdullah and I spent six days together in Grenada. Revolution was still in the air. One afternoon, as I was scribbling notes on my battered clipboard, a man approached us. He asked me where I was from. I asked him why he wanted to know, and Abdullah and I resumed our conversation.

But not for long. Suddenly, other men approached.

Abdullah, who must have realized what was happening, began sidling off in another direction. But it was too late. Yet providence was kind; the threatening cordon gave way to Police Superintendent Jerome Honoré, who addressed us courteously and identified himself. His cultivated manner and French accent made me feel as if I were chatting with a Sorbonne professor, not an officer of the law.

Vaguely, I remember what I was later told about Superintendent Honoré. Several years earlier, he had resigned from Grenada's police force because of his disenchantment with the Gairy administration. After the revolution, he had rejoined the force. It was a good thing for us that he had. He asked me what we were doing in Grenada. I explained that I was writing a biography of Malcolm X. I also explained why I had chosen to interview Abdullah in Grenada. Mr. Honoré apologized to us, but told us we had to come to police headquarters. Since Abdullah was scheduled to return to Guyana the following day, I asked Honoré if he would allow us to stay together, so that I could continue interviewing Abdullah at police headquarters. He assured me that we would not be separated.

As I recall, police headquarters was located in or very near the massive stone fort that lies atop the hill overlooking the lovely harbor of St. George's, Grenada's capital. Few suspected spies receive the courteous welcome that awaited us there. We joked with the secretaries. We continued the interview; that is, until Abdullah was taken into another room for questioning.

The police released us after questioning me. Since the stores were about to close and Abdullah wanted to purchase some things that he needed to take back to Guyana (where most manufactured items are prohibitively expensive), Honoré drove us downtown in his own car. As we shook hands and parted, he apologized once more. After I returned to the U.S., I often wondered what happened to him, and whether he was harmed by America's bullylike

1983 invasion of the virtually defenseless, tiny island. About a year ago, I was relieved to learn he is well.

More than ten years have elapsed since Abdullah and I parted company and left Grenada. At intervals, we communicate, as best we can, by mail. Some time ago, he sent me several tape-recorded speeches, portions of which appear in this book. Its subject needs no introduction, for Malcolm X was the standard-bearer for an entire generation of Black militants. He was anathema to most American whites, at least until his martyrdom and the publication of his best-selling autobiography. But even his detractors acknowledge that he was one of the foremost American political figures and political orators of the mid-twentieth century.

This collection of Malcolm's speeches is the result of a team effort. Pathfinder Press has its political views and I have mine, which differ substantially. Pathfinder's political assessment of Malcolm is also different from mine. But one thing we do agree about is that Malcolm's views should be heard.

Hence this book. With Abdullah's help and the help of others, I have provided the tape recordings of Malcolm's speeches and the editorial commentary preceding each section. Pathfinder has provided the money for publication. It has also prepared the written transcripts of each tape recording and has done nearly all the real editing.

Publisher's foreword

HAVING long been an uncompromising fighter for Black rights and foe of Washington's imperialist policies abroad, Malcolm X went through a rapid political evolution to carefully thought-out anticapitalist and, then, prosocialist positions during the last year of his life. That process was cut short by his brutal assassination on February 21, 1965.

This political evolution places the works of Malcolm X on Pathfinder's list of published writings and speeches alongside those of Fidel Castro, Ernesto Che Guevara, Maurice Bishop, Nelson Mandela, Thomas Sankara, and Carlos Fonseca. These leaders, too, each in their particular way, traveled the road through hard-fought national liberation struggles to broader internationalist perspectives and revolutionary action. In doing so, they led millions of workers and farmers in changing the world.

This has been a clear pattern of the world revolution since World War II. Malcolm X is thus far the outstanding representative of this pattern to emerge from the working class in the United States.

Because of the importance of Malcolm X's ideas and activity to the renewal of revolutionary leadership on a world scale, Pathfinder moved quickly following his assassination in February 1965 to publish the writings and speeches in which he presented his rapidly evolving views. This publishing effort produced *Two Speeches by*

Malcolm X (1965), *Malcolm X Talks to Young People* (1965), *Malcolm X Speaks* (1965), *Malcolm X on Afro-American History* (1967), *By Any Means Necessary: Speeches, Interviews and a Letter by Malcolm X* (1970), and more recently the Spanish-language *Habla Malcolm X* (1984). These books largely exhausted the pool of writings and speeches by Malcolm from this period that were known to be available for publication.

Understandably, then, Pathfinder was pleased to be approached by Dr. Bruce Perry to publish several speeches and interviews that he had tracked down (by efforts described in his introduction to this volume) while writing a biography of Malcolm X that is scheduled to be published in 1990. Some of these items were transcribed from tape recordings obtained from James 67X Shabazz. Shabazz was a co-leader with Malcolm X of the Muslim Mosque, Inc., and Organization of Afro-American Unity (OAAU).

There are no startling revelations in these new materials.* They do not appreciably alter the political legacy left by Malcolm X, nor could they. Like other great modern revolutionists, Malcolm sought a wide variety of platforms from which to explain his ideas to the widest possible public. And he sought to collaborate with and learn from others who were thinking and acting as revolutionists. Malcolm X's views can be read and studied in the collections cited above.

---

* The one partial exception is the important new information presented by Malcolm X in a February 15, 1965, speech about the secret negotiations he entered into at the initiative of Nation of Islam leader Elijah Muhammad with leaders of the racist and ultrarightist Ku Klux Klan. While these matters had been noted in passing in press coverage at the time, and are referred to in Peter Goldman's *The Death and Life of Malcolm X* (New York: Harper & Row, 1974), what Malcolm X himself—from the standpoint of a direct participant in these talks—actually said about them on the only occasion that he publicly discussed this matter has never before been in print.

At the same time, the new materials collected here are not just "more speeches" by Malcolm X. This volume includes two of his last public speeches, given during the final week of his life. One was delivered in Harlem on February 15 to a meeting of the Organization of Afro-American Unity; the other the following night to an audience in Rochester, New York. Two other items are important interviews from December 1964 that shed light on how Malcolm X began to articulate the evolution of his thinking in light of experiences during his second extended trip to the Middle East and Africa from July through November of that year.

It is easier to understand the development of Malcolm X's political perspectives during his final months by knowing something about the far-reaching conclusions he had already come to prior to his public break with the Nation of Islam in March 1964. Both the continuity and change are illuminated in two speeches, from early and late 1963, that are published here for the first time.

Many views that Malcolm X maintained to his dying day are presented powerfully in these 1963 speeches: steadfast opposition to Jim Crow segregation; fierce pride in the African roots of Black people; refusal to speak about himself as an "American" or about the U.S. government and armed forces as "our" government and "our" army; emphasis on the need to look at all events "in the international context"; recognition of the Democratic and Republican parties as organizations of the racist and imperialist oppressors; support for the right of self-defense against racist terror, including armed self-defense where necessary; identification with national liberation struggles throughout Africa, Asia, and the Americas; repudiation of the illusion that justice can ever be advanced by relying on the good-heartedness of the oppressors and exploiters, or some common humanity shared with them.

At the same time, reading these 1963 speeches in conjunction with the 1964 interviews and the two 1965 public talks serves to underline the changes that his political views had undergone in the months prior to the assassination. The reader will learn firsthand about Malcolm X's political evolution on a broad range of questions:

1. *Who are the racist oppressors.* In 1963 Malcolm X expressed the view that the "black, brown, red, and yellow" peoples of the earth "had an oppressor in common, an exploiter in common—the European," that is, whites, regardless of their deeds. In his Rochester speech, on February 16, 1965, he presented a different view:

"We don't judge a man because of the color of his skin. We don't judge you because you're white; we don't judge you because you're black; we don't judge you because you're brown. We judge you because of what you do and what you practice.... So we're not against people because they're white. But we're against those who practice racism. We're against those who drop bombs on people because their color happens to be of a different shade than yours."

2. *Anti-imperialism.* During his final months, Malcolm X began to present a clear explanation of who he had in mind in speaking of "those who practice racism" and "those who drop bombs on people because [of] their color."

In his December 27, 1964, radio interview, Malcolm X hailed those United Nations representatives who were "openly accusing the United States," as well as the European colonial powers, "of being an imperialist power and of practicing racism." In his Harlem speech on February 15, 1965, he expanded on this theme. "There's a worldwide revolution going on," Malcolm said. "[W]hat is it revolting against? The power structure.... An international power structure consisting of American interests, French interests, English interests, Belgian interests, European interests.... A structure, a house that has ruled the world up until now."

3. *Internationalism and Black liberation.* The evolution in Malcolm X's views on these matters led him to new

political conclusions about the road forward for Black liberation. In his Rochester speech he summarized the position he had come to during the previous several months:

"Any kind of movement for freedom of Black people based solely within the confines of America is absolutely doomed to fail. . . . So one of the first steps that we became involved in, those of us who got into the Organization of Afro-American Unity, was to come up with a program that would make our grievances international and make the world see that our problem was no longer a Negro problem or an American problem but a human problem. A problem for humanity. And a problem that should be attacked by all elements of humanity."

(Malcolm X's views on marriages between Blacks and whites were another reflection of his evolving internationalism and changing outlook on who is responsible for racist oppression. In the January 23, 1963, speech published here and in others given during that earlier period, Malcolm put substantial emphasis on the Nation of Islam's opposition to such marriages. During the last months of his life Malcolm publicly changed his opinion. In a January 1965 interview cited in *Malcolm X Speaks* [p. 197], he explained: "I believe in recognizing every human being as a human being—neither white, black, brown, or red; and when you are dealing with humanity as a family there's no question of integration or intermarriage. It's just one human being marrying another human being, or one human being living around and with another human being. I may say, though, that . . . I don't think the burden to defend any position should ever be put upon the black man, because it is the white man collectively who has shown that he is hostile toward integration and toward intermarriage and toward these other strides toward oneness.")

4. *Political action.* Those who had split away from the Nation of Islam, Malcolm explained in the Rochester

speech, "were the real activists of the movement who were intelligent enough to want some kind of program that would enable us to fight for the rights of all Black people here in the Western Hemisphere." In the Nation, he said, "[B]ecause we were never permitted to take part in politics, we were in a vacuum politically. We were in a religious vacuum; we were in a political vacuum. We were actually alienated, cut off from all type of activity with even the world that we were fighting against. We became sort of a religious-political hybrid, all to ourselves. Not involved in anything but just standing on the sidelines condemning everything. But in no position to correct anything because we couldn't take action.

"Yet at the same time, the nature of the movement was such that it attracted the activists," Malcolm X explained. "Those who wanted action. Those who wanted to do something about the evils that confronted all Black people."

5. *Civil rights struggles.* This shift toward political action changed the approach taken by Malcolm X to the mass civil rights movement that, through a decade of hard-fought and bloody battles, succeeded in battering down the Jim Crow system of segregation by the mid-1960s. In his October 1963 speech he was still referring to this movement in largely derisive terms. For example, he spoke of the mass August 1963 civil rights mobilization of 250,000 people in the U.S. capital as "the recent ridiculous march on Washington."

In his February 15, 1965, speech, however, Malcolm X explained that the U.S. government was so upset about his break from the Nation of Islam because "all those militants who formerly were in it and were held in check would immediately become involved in the civil rights struggle, and they would add the same kinds of energy to the civil rights struggle that they gave to the Black Muslim movement."

Malcolm X himself had just returned from the civil

rights encampment in Selma, Alabama. As he told the audience in his Harlem speech to the OAAU, "I promised the brothers and sisters in Alabama when I was there that we'd be back. I'll be back, you'll be back, we'll be back."

6. *Religion and political organization.* These conclusions convinced Malcolm X that—while he himself remained a devout and practicing Muslim and continued his work in the Muslim Mosque, Inc.—a new kind of independent and secular political organization had to be constructed. This organization had to be open to all Blacks, regardless of religious or other secular beliefs, who agreed on the need to organize a fight around common political goals. Even while still in the Nation of Islam, he said in the Rochester speech, those who shared his dissatisfaction had become less and less "concerned with the religion of the Black man. Because whether he was a Methodist or a Baptist or an atheist or an agnostic, he caught the same hell."

With this in mind, the Organization of Afro-American Unity was launched in June 1964. The OAAU, as Malcolm X explained in the Rochester speech, "is a nonreligious organization . . . structured organizationally to allow for active participation of any Afro-American, any Black American, in a program that is designed to eliminate the negative political, economic, and social evils that our people are confronted by in this society."

7. *Women's political and social advancement.* Just as Malcolm X's evolving perspective necessitated reaching out to fellow fighters on a political basis regardless of their views on religious matters, it also meant recognizing the need to involve women on an equal footing in the battles. In his 1963 speeches, Malcolm X was still presenting a view of women as subordinate to men, with their place restricted to hearth and home. By December 1964, however, he had this to say:

"One thing I noticed in both the Middle East and Africa,

in every country that was progressive, the women were progressive. In every country that was underdeveloped and backward, it was to the same degree that the women were undeveloped, or underdeveloped, and backward. . . . [I]t's noticeable that in these type of societies where they put the woman in a closet and discourage her from getting a sufficient education and don't give her the incentive by allowing her maximum participation in whatever area of the society where she's qualified, they kill her incentive. . . . So in the African countries where they opt for mass education, whether it be male or female, you find that they have a more valid society, a more progressive society."

Many other examples of Malcolm X's political evolution can be traced through these pages. Readers will also need to go to other collections of his writings and speeches to learn about the development of his views on a number of additional important matters: his growing anticapitalism, his decision in the last months of his life to no longer define his viewpoint as "Black nationalism," the question of alliances between political organizations of Blacks such as the OAAU and other organizations of the oppressed and exploited.

The speeches collected for this volume by Bruce Perry, then, make an important addition to our knowledge of the political ideas of Malcolm X and the experiences that shaped their development. The importance of making this material available was well explained some twenty-three years ago at a March 1965 memorial meeting for Malcolm X sponsored by the Militant Labor Forum in New York City. Appropriately, the speaker was James 67X Shabazz, who provided a number of the speeches published here.[*] Shabazz said:

"Malcolm's body lies in a grave. His words lie neatly

---

[*] Shabazz's speech was printed in the March 15, 1965, issue of the *Mil-*

couched on papers and mysteriously captured on recording tapes, but Malcolm's thoughts, like invisible seeds, have been planted in the minds of oppressed peoples in America, in Africa, in the Middle East, and in Europe. And many men in different places, at different times, and in different languages will clothe these thoughts in the garments that are necessary for them to fit the different conditions. Malcolm's thoughts will only die when all people—especially of African origin—are free as Malcolm wanted us to be."

Steve Clark
February 1989

---

itant newsweekly published in New York. Excerpts from a speech by Jack Barnes given at the same meeting are available in *Malcolm X Talks to Young People*, published by Pathfinder.

Chronology

May 19, 1925	Malcolm Little born in Omaha, Nebraska
February 1946	Sentenced in Massachusetts to 8-10 years imprisonment for burglary; serves 6½ years
1948-1949	Conversion to Islam
August 1952	Paroled from prison
1953	Having renamed himself "Malcolm X," he becomes an assistant minister of the Nation of Islam's Temple Number 1, located in Detroit
June 1954	Becomes minister of Harlem, New York, temple
1959	First trip to the Middle East and Africa
April 1963	Confronts Elijah Muhammad about his adultery
December 1963-February 1964	Elijah Muhammad orders Malcolm to remain silent, allegedly because of his barbed, unauthorized remarks about President Kennedy's assassination. Malcolm becomes isolated within his own movement
March 1964	Announces founding of Muslim Mosque, Inc.
April-May 1964	Second trip to Africa and the Middle East
June 1964	First public meeting of the Organization of Afro-American Unity
July-November 1964	Third trip to Africa
February 14, 1965	A firebomb lays waste to Malcolm's home
February 21, 1965	Assassinated in New York City

PART 1

Two 1963 university speeches

By 1963, the differences between Malcolm and Elijah Muhammad had come to a head. But Malcolm chose, for a variety of personal and political reasons, not to leave the Nation of Islam. In January, he spoke at Michigan State University. Throughout his speech, which attested to his unique ability to captivate the very whites he pilloried, he repeatedly stressed that the views he was presenting were Mr. Muhammad's. He said: "Now, in . . . professing to speak for Black people by representing the Honorable Elijah Muhammad. . . ."

In October, Malcolm spoke at the University of California at Berkeley. Over and over, he stated that the views he was presenting were those of Mr. Muhammad, whom he characterized as a "modern Moses." But the exaggerated praise masked secret opposition. Fear that the opposition might become open prompted Mr. Muhammad, in early December, to use Malcolm's unauthorized remarks about President Kennedy's assassination as an excuse to forbid him from making any more public statements. Malcolm had characterized the assassination as a case of "chickens coming home to roost."

At Harlem rally, 1963.
(Photo: Robert Haggins)

Twenty million Black people in a political, economic, and mental prison

IT SHOULD be pointed out at the outset that I represent the Honorable Elijah Muhammad, whose followers are known as the Muslims here in America and actually are the fastest growing group—fastest growing religious group—among Black people anywhere in the Western Hemisphere. And it is our intention to try and spell out what the philosophy and aims and motivations of the Honorable Elijah Muhammad happen to be and his solution to this very serious problem that America finds herself confronted with.

And I might point out, too, that if you don't think that the problem is serious, then you need only to listen to the attorney general, Robert F. Kennedy. In almost every speech he's been involved in, especially during the past few months and even today, he has pointed out that the race problem is America's most serious domestic problem. And since the problem is so serious, it's time to take some serious steps to get to the factors that create this problem.

And again I want to thank the African Students Association and the campus NAACP for displaying the unity necessary to bring a very controversial issue before the students here on campus. The unity of Africans abroad and the unity of Africans here in this country can bring about practically any kind of achievement or accomplishment that Black people want today.

When I say the Africans abroad and the Africans here in this country—the man that you call Negro is nothing but an African himself. Why, some of them have been brainwashed into thinking that Africa is a place with no culture, no history, no contribution to civilization or science. So many of these Negroes, they take offense when they're identified with their homeland. But today we want to point out the different types of Negroes that you have to deal with. Then once you know there's more than one type, then you won't come up with just one type solution.

And to point out how timely the invitation is or was—I don't want to read newspapers to you, but in the *Detroit News* dated Thursday, January 17, it told about the Interfaith Council of Religion that was held in Chicago last week. And the topic of their conversation was the race problem here in America. And it pointed out that all of the time that they spent and money that they spent, actually they didn't get to the meat of the issue. And in this particular copy of the paper, on page three, the chaplain at Wayne State University actually criticized the efforts of these Protestants, Catholics, and Jews in Chicago last week for failing to bring spokesmen to that conference who really would speak for Black people and spell out issues that were not being spelled out by the others.

And I just want to read a recommendation that he made. Mr. [Malcolm] Boyd believes that the conference might have accomplished much good if the speakers had included a white supremacist and a Negro race leader, preferably a top man in the American Black Muslim movement. He said that a debate between them would undoubtedly be bitter, but it would accomplish one thing. It would get some of the real issues out into the open. And I think that the man is right. Most of the so-called Negroes that you listen to on the race problem usually don't represent any following of Black people. Usually they are Negroes who have been put in that position by the white man himself. And when they speak they're not speaking for Black people, they're saying exactly what they know the white man who put them in that position wants to hear them say.

So again, I think that it was very progressive and objective on the part of these two sponsoring groups to give us an opportunity to tell you how Black people really think and how Black people really feel and how dissatisfied Black people have become—increasingly so—with the conditions that our people find ourselves in here in this country.

Now in speaking as a—professing to speak for Black people by representing the Honorable Elijah Muhammad, you want to know who does he represent. Who does he speak for? There are two types of Negroes in this country. There's the bourgeois type who blinds himself to the condition of his people, and who is satisfied with token solutions. He's in the minority. He's a handful. He's usually the handpicked Negro who benefits from token integration. But the masses of Black people who really suffer the brunt of brutality and the conditions that exist in this country are represented by the leadership of the Honorable Elijah Muhammad.

So when I come in here to speak to you, I'm not coming in here speaking as a Baptist or a Methodist or a Democrat or a Republican or a Christian or a Jew or—not even as an American. Because if I stand up here—if I could stand up here and speak to you as an American we wouldn't have anything to talk about. The problem would be solved. So we don't even profess to speak as an American. We are speaking as—I am speaking as a Black man. And I'm letting you know how a Black man thinks, how a Black man feels, and how dissatisfied Black men should have been 400 years ago. So, and if I raise my voice you'll forgive me or excuse me, I'm not doing it out of disrespect. I'm speaking from my heart, and you get it exactly as the feeling brings it out.

When I pointed out that there are two kinds of Negroes—some Negroes don't want a Black man to speak for them. That type of Negro doesn't even want to be Black. He's ashamed of being Black. And you'll never hear him refer to himself as Black. Now that type we don't pretend to speak for. You can speak for him. In fact you can have him. [*Laughter*]

But the ones that the Honorable Elijah Muhammad speaks for are those whose pattern of thinking, pattern of thought, pattern of behavior, pattern of action is being changed by what the Honorable Elijah Muhammad is teaching throughout America. These are that mass element, and usually when you hear the press refer to the Honorable Elijah Muhammad, they refer to him as a teacher of hate or an advocator of violence or—what's this other thing?—Black supremacist.

Actually this is the type of propaganda put together by the press, thinking that this will alienate masses of Black people from what he's saying. But actually the only one whom that type of propaganda alienates is this Negro who's always up in your face begging you for what you have or begging you for a chance to live in your neighborhood or work on your job or marry one of your women. Well that type of Negro naturally doesn't want to hear what the Honorable Elijah Muhammad is talking about. But the type that wants to hear what he's saying is the type who feels that he'll get farther by standing on his own feet and doing something for himself towards solving his own problem, instead of accusing you of creating the problem and then, at the same time, depending upon you to do something to solve the problem.

So you have two types of Negro. The old type and the new type. Most of you know the old type. When you read about him in history during slavery he was called "Uncle Tom." He was the house Negro. And during slavery you had two Negroes. You had the house Negro and the field

Negro. The house Negro usually lived close to his master. He dressed like his master. He wore his master's second-hand clothes. He ate food that his master left on the table. And he lived in his master's house—probably in the basement or the attic—but he still lived in the master's house. So whenever that house Negro identified himself, he always identified himself in the same sense that his master identified himself.

When his master said, "We have good food," the house Negro would say, "Yes, we have plenty of good food." "We" have plenty of good food. When the master said that "we have a fine home here," the house Negro said, "Yes, we have a fine home here." When the master would be sick, the house Negro identified himself so much with his master he'd say, "What's the matter boss, we sick?" His master's pain was his pain. And it hurt him more for his master to be sick than for him to be sick himself. When the house started burning down, that type of Negro would fight harder to put the master's house out than the master himself would.

But then you had another Negro out in the field. The house Negro was in the minority. The masses—the field Negroes were the masses. They were in the majority. When the master got sick, they prayed that he'd die. [*Laughter*] If his house caught on fire, they'd pray for a wind to come along and fan the breeze.

If someone came to the house Negro and said, "Let's go, let's separate," naturally that Uncle Tom would say, "Go where? What could I do without boss? Where would I live? How would I dress? Who would look out for me?" That's the house Negro. But if you went to the field Negro and said, "Let's go, let's separate," he wouldn't even ask you where or how. He'd say, "Yes, let's go." And that one ended right there.

So today you have a twentieth-century-type of house Negro. A twentieth-century Uncle Tom. He's just as much an Uncle Tom today as Uncle Tom was 100 or 200 years ago. Only he's a modern Uncle Tom. That Uncle Tom wore a handkerchief around his head. This Uncle Tom wears a top hat. He's sharp. He dresses just like you do. He speaks the same phraseology, the same language. He tries to speak it better than you do. He speaks with the same accents, same diction. And when you say, "your army," he says, "our army." He hasn't got anybody to defend him, but anytime you say "we" he says "we." "Our president," "our government," "our Senate," "our congressmen," "our this and our that." And he hasn't even got a seat in that "our" even at the end of the line. So this is the twentieth-century Negro. Whenever you say "you," the personal pronoun in the singular or in the plural, he uses it right along with you. When you say you're in trouble, he says, "Yes, we're in trouble."

But there's another kind of Black man on the scene. If you say you're in trouble, he says, "Yes, you're in trouble." [*Laughter*] He doesn't identify himself with your plight whatsoever.

And this is the thing that the white people in America have got to come to realize. That there are two types of Black people in this country. One who identifies with you so much so he will let you brutalize him and still beg you for a chance to sit next to you. And then there's one who's not interested in sitting next to you. He's not interested in being around you. He's not interested in what you have. He wants something of his own. He wants to sit someplace where he can call his own. He doesn't want a seat in your restaurant where you can give him some old bad coffee or bad food. He wants his own restaurant. And he wants some land where he can build that restaurant on, in a city that it can go in. He wants something of his own.

And when you realize that this type of thinking is existing and developing fastly or swiftly behind the teachings of the Honorable Elijah Muhammad among the so-called Negroes, then I think that you'll also realize that this whole phony effort at integration is no solution. Because the most you can do with this phony effort toward integration is to put out some token integration. And whereas this Uncle Tom will accept your token effort, the masses of Black people in this country are no more interested in token integration than they would be if you offered them a chance to sit inside a furnace somewhere. The only one who'll do that is this twentieth-century Uncle Tom. And you can always tell him because he wants to be next to you. He wants to eat with you. He wants to sleep with you. He wants to marry your woman, marry your mother, marry your sister, marry your daughter. And if you watch him close enough he's even after your wife. [*Laughter*]

This type has blind faith—in your religion. He's not interested in any religion of his own. He believes in a white Jesus, white Mary, white angels, and he's trying to get to a white heaven. When you listen to him in his church singing, he sings a song, I think they call it, "Wash me white as snow." He wants to be—he wants to be turned white so he can go to heaven with a white man. It's not his fault; it's actually not his fault. But this is the state of his mind. This is the result of 400 years of brainwashing here in America. You have taken a man who is black on the outside and made him white on the inside. His brain is white as snow. His heart is white as snow. And therefore, whenever you say, this is ours, he thinks he's white the same as you, so what's yours he thinks is also his. Even right on down to your woman.

Now many of them will take offense at my implying that he wants your woman. They'll say, "No, this is what Bill Bowen, Talmadge, and all of the White Citizens' Councils say." They say that to fool you. If this is not what they want, watch them. And if you find evidence to the contrary, then I'll take back my words. But all you have to do is give him the chance to get near you, and you'll find that he is not satisfied until he is sitting next to your woman, or closer to her than that.

And this type of Negro, usually he hates Black and loves white. He doesn't want to be Black, he wants to be white. And he'll get on his bended knees and beg you for integration, which means he would rather live—rather than live with his own kind who love him, he'll force himself to live in neighborhoods around white people whom he knows don't mean him any good. And again I say, this is not his fault. He is sick. And as long as America listens to this sick Negro, who is begging to be integrated into American society despite the fact that the attitude and actions of whites are sufficient proof that he is not wanted, why then you are actually allowing him to force you into a position where you look just as sick as he looks.

If someone holds a gun on a white man and makes him embrace me—put his hand, arm, around me—this isn't love nor is it brotherhood. What they are doing is forcing the white man to be a hypocrite, to practice hypocrisy. But if that white man will put his arm around me willingly, voluntarily, of his own volition, then that's love, that's brotherhood, that's a solution to the problem.

Likewise, as long as the government has to get out here and legislate to force Negroes into a white neighborhood or force Negroes into a white school or force Negroes into white industry—and make white people pretend that they go for this—all the government is doing is making white people be hypocrites. And rather than be classified as a bigot, by putting a block, the average white person actually would rather put up a hypocritical face, the face of a hypocrite, than to tell the Black man, "No, you stay over there and let me stay over here." So that's no solution.

As long as you force people to act in a hypocritical way, you will never solve their problem. It has to be—the Honorable Elijah Muhammad teaches us that a solution has to be devised that will be satisfactory, completely satisfactory to the Black man and completely satisfactory to the white man. And the only thing that makes white people completely satisfied and Black people completely satisfied, when they're in their right mind, is when the Black man has his own and the white man has his own. You have what you need; we have what we need. Then both of us have something, and even the Bible says, "God bless the child that has his own." And the poor so-called Negro doesn't have his own name, doesn't have his own language, doesn't have his own culture, doesn't have his own history. He doesn't have his own country. He doesn't even have his own mind. And he thinks that he's Black 'cause God cursed him. He's not Black 'cause God cursed him. He's Black because—rather he's cursed because he's out of his mind. He has lost his mind. He has a white mind instead of the type of mind that he should have.

So, when these so-called Negroes who want integration try and force themselves into the white society, which doesn't solve the problem—the Honorable Elijah Muhammad teaches us that that type of Negro is the one that creates the problem. And the type of white person who perpetuates the problem is the one who poses as a liberal and pretends that the Negro should be integrated, as long as he integrates someone else's neighborhood. But all these whites that you see running around here talking about how liberal they are, and we believe everybody should have what they want and go where they want and do what they want, as soon as a Negro moves into that white liberal's neighborhood, that white liberal is—well he moves out faster than the white bigot from Mississippi, Alabama, and from someplace else.

So we won't solve the problem listening to that Uncle Tom Negro, and the problem won't be solved listening to the so-called white liberal. The only time the problem is going to be solved is when a Black man can sit down like a Black man and a white man can sit down like a white man. And make no excuses whatsoever with each other in discussing the problem. No offense will stem from factors that are brought up. But both of them have to sit down like men, on one side and on the other side, and look at it in terms of Black and white. And then take some kind of solution based upon the factors that we see, rather than upon that which we would like to believe.

And when I said that this Negro wants to force his way into the white man's family, this integrationist-minded Negro wants to force his way into the white man's family, some don't believe that. Some take issue with that. But you take all of the integrationists, all of those who are used to finance the program of the integrationists, the average so-called Negro celebrity, put all of them in one pile. And as fast as you name them off, you'll find that every one of them is married either to a white woman or a white man. From Lena Horne, Eartha Kitt, Sammy Davis, and you could name 'em all night long, they—although they say that this is not what we want—that's what they've done. That's what they have. And we don't—the Black masses don't want what Lena Horne wants or what Sammy Davis wants or what who's-his-name, the rest of them want.

Usually you'll find that before Sammy Davis and Lena Horne and Eartha Kitt and Harry Belafonte become involved in a mixed marriage you could go into the Negro community, any one across the country, and find those stars with records on the jukeboxes in the Negro community. You can't walk into a Negro community today and find anybody that the Negro community knows is involved in a mixed marriage with their records being popular in the Negro community. Subconsciously a Negro doesn't have any respect or regard or confidence, nor can he be moved by, another Black man, a Black man who marries a white woman or a Black woman who marries a white man.

And when they put out that picture to you that all of us want your woman, no, just that twentieth-century Uncle

Tom. He wants her. But, then when you fulfill—think you're going to solve your problem by pleasing him, you're only making the problem worse. You have to go back and listen to the problem as it is presented by the masses of Black people, not by these handpicked, handful of Uncle Toms who benefit from token integration.

Also this type of so-called Negro, by being intoxicated over the white man, he never sees beyond the white man. He never sees beyond America. He never looks at himself or where he fits into things on the world stage. He only can see himself here in America, on the American stage or the white stage, where the white man is in the majority, where the white man is the boss. So this type of Negro always feels like he's outnumbered or he's the underdog or he's the minority. And it puts him in the role of a beggar—a cowardly, humble, Uncle Tomming beggar on anything that he says is—that should be his by right. [*Commotion*]

Whereas there is—he wants to be an American rather than to be Black. He wants to be something other than what he is. And knowing that America is a white country, he knows he can't be Black and be an American too. So he never calls himself Black. He calls himself an American Negro—a Negro in America. And usually he'll deny his own race, his own color, just to be a second-class American. He'll deny his own history, his own culture. He'll deny all of his brothers and sisters in Africa, in Asia, in the East, just to be a second-class American. He denies everything that he represents or everything that was in his past, just to be accepted into a country and into a government that has rejected him ever since he was brought here.

For this Negro is sick. He has to be sick to try and force himself amongst some people who don't want him, or to be accepted into a government that has used its entire political system and educational system to keep him relegated to the role of a second-class citizen. Therefore he spends a lifetime begging for acceptance into the same government that made slaves of his people. He gives his life for a country that made his people slaves and still confines them to the role of second-class citizens. And we feel that he wastes his time begging white politicians, political hypocrites, for civil rights or for some kind of first-class citizenship.

He is like a watchdog or a hound dog. You may run into a dog—no matter how vicious a dog is, you find him out in the street, he won't bite you. But when you get him up on the porch, he will growl, he'll take your leg. Now that dog, when he's out in the street, only his own life is threatened, and he's never been trained to protect himself. He's only been trained by his master to think in terms of what's good for his master. So when you catch him in the street and you threaten him, he'll go around you. But when you come up on the—through the gate when he's sitting on the master's porch, then he'll bare his fangs and get ready to bite you. Not because you're threatening him, but because you threaten his master who has trained him not to protect himself but to protect the property of the master.

And this type of twentieth-century Uncle Tom is the same way. He'll never attack you, but he'll attack me. I can run into him out on the street and blast him; he won't say a word. But if I look like I'm about to blast you in here, he'll open up his mouth and put up a better defense for you than you can put up for yourself. Because he hasn't been trained to defend himself. He has only been trained to open up his mouth in defense of his master. He hasn't been educated, he's been trained. When a man is educated, he can think for himself and defend himself and speak for himself. But this twentieth-century Uncle Tom Negro never opens up his mouth in defense of a Black man. He opens up his mouth in defense of the white man, in defense of America, in defense of the American government. He doesn't even know where his government is, because he doesn't know that he ever had one. He doesn't know where his country is, because he doesn't know that he ever had one.

He believes in exactly what he was taught in school. That when he was kidnapped by the white man, he was a savage in the jungle someplace eating people and throwing spears and with a bone in his nose. And the average American Negro has that concept of the African continent. It is not his fault. This is what has been given to him by the American educational system.

He doesn't realize that there were civilizations and cultures on the African continent at a time when the people in Europe were crawling around in the caves, going naked. He doesn't realize that the Black man in Africa was wearing silk, was wearing slippers—that he was able to spin himself, make himself at a time when the people up in Europe were going naked.

He doesn't realize that he was living in palaces on the African continent when the people in Europe were living in caves. He doesn't realize that he was living in a civilization in Africa where science had been so far advanced, especially even the astronomical sciences, to a point where Africans could plot the course of the stars in the universe when the people up in Europe still thought the earth was round, the planet was round—or flat.

He doesn't realize the advancement and the high state of his own culture that he was living in before he was kidnapped and brought to this country by the white man. He knows nothing about that. He knows nothing about the ancient Egyptian civilization on the African continent. Or the ancient Carthaginian civilization on the African continent. Or the ancient civilizations of Mali on the African continent. Civilizations that were highly developed and produced scientists. Timbuktu, the center of the Mali Empire, was the center of learning at a time when the people up in Europe didn't even know what a book was. He doesn't know this, because he hasn't been taught. And because he doesn't know this, when you mention Africa to him, why he thinks you're talking about a jungle.

And I went to Africa in 1959 and didn't see any jungle. And I didn't see any mud huts until I got back to Harlem in New York City. [*Laughter and applause*]

So you're familiar with that type of Negro. And the Black man that you're not familiar with is the one that we would like to point out now.

He is the new—he is the new type. He is the type that the white man seldom ever comes in contact with. And when you do come in contact with him, you're shocked, because you didn't know that this type of Black man existed. And immediately you think, well here's one of those Black supremacists or racists or extremists who believe in violence and all of that kind of—well that's what they call it. [*Laughter*]

This new type of Black man, he doesn't want integration; he wants separation. Not segregation, separation. To him, segregation, as we're taught by the Honorable Elijah Muhammad, means that which is forced upon inferiors by superiors. A segregated community is a Negro community. But the white community, though it's all white, is never called a segregated community. It's a separate community. In the white community, the white man controls the economy, his own economy, his own politics, his own everything. That's his community. But at the same time while the Negro lives in a separate community, it's a segregated community. Which means its regulated from the outside by outsiders. The white man has all of the businesses in the Negro community. He runs the politics of the Negro community. He controls all the civic organizations in the Negro community. This is a segregated community.

We don't go for segregation. We go for separation. Separation is when you have your own. You control your own economy; you control your own politics; you control your own society; you control your own everything. You have yours and you control yours; we have ours and we control ours.

They don't call Chinatown in New York City or on the West Coast a segregated community, yet it's all Chinese. But the Chinese control it. Chinese voluntarily live there, they control it. They run it. They have their own schools. They control their own politics, control their own industry. And they don't feel like they're being made inferior because they have to live to themselves. They choose to live to themselves. They live there voluntarily. And they are doing for themselves in their community the same thing you do for yourself in your community. This makes them equal because they have what you have. But if they didn't have what you have, then they'd be controlled from your side; even though they would be on their side, they'd be controlled from your side by you.

So when we who follow the Honorable Elijah Muhammad say that we're for separation, it should be emphasized we're not for segregation; we're for separation. We want the same for ourselves as you have for yourself. And when we get it, then it's possible to think more intelligently and to think in terms that are along peaceful lines. But a man who doesn't have what is his, he can never think always in terms that are along peaceful lines.

This new type rejects the white man's Christian religion. He recognizes the real enemy. That Uncle Tom can't see his enemy. He thinks his friend is his enemy and his enemy is his friend. And he usually ends up loving his enemy, turning his other cheek to his enemy. But this new type, he doesn't turn the other cheek to anybody. He doesn't believe in any kind of peaceful suffering. He believes in obeying the law. He believes in respecting people. He believes in doing unto others as he would have done to himself. But at the same time, if anybody attacks him, he believes in retaliating if it costs him his life. And it is good for white people to know this. Because if white people get the impression that Negroes all endorse this old turn-the-other-cheek cowardly philosophy of Dr. Martin Luther King, then whites are going to make the mistake of putting their hands on some Black man, thinking that he's going to turn the other cheek, and he'll end up losing his hand and losing his life in the try. [*Commotion and laughter*]

So it is always better to let someone know where you stand. And there are a large number of Black people in this country who don't endorse any phase of what Dr. Martin Luther King and these other twentieth-century religious Uncle Toms are putting in front of the public eye to make it look like this is the way, this is the behavior, or this is the thought pattern of most of our people.

Also this new type, you'll find, he doesn't look upon it as being any honor to be in America. He knows he didn't come here on the *Mayflower.* He knows he was brought here in a slave ship. But this twentieth-century Uncle Tom, he'll stand up in your face and tell you about when his fathers landed on Plymouth Rock. His father never landed on Plymouth Rock; the rock was dropped on him [*Laughter*] but he wasn't dropped on it. [*Applause*]

So this type doesn't make any apology for being in America, nor does he make any apology for the problem his presence in America presents for Uncle Sam. He knows he was brought here in chains, and he knows he was brought here against his will. He knows that the problem itself was created by the white man and that it was created because the white man brought us here in chains against our will. It was a crime. And the one who committed that crime is the criminal today who should pay for the crime that was committed. You don't put the crime in jail, you put the criminal in jail. And kidnapping is a crime. Slavery is a crime. Lynching is a crime. And the presence of 20 million Black people in America against their will is a living witness, a living testimony of the crime that Uncle Sam committed, your forefathers committed, when our people were brought here in chains.

And the reason the problem can't be solved today is you try and dress it up and doctor it up and make it look like a favor was done to the Black man by having brought the Black man here. But when you realize that it was a crime that was committed, then you approach the solution to that problem in a different light and then you can probably solve it. And as long as you think Negroes are running around here of the opinion that you're doing them a favor by letting them have some of this and letting them have some of that, why naturally every time you give a little bit more justice or freedom to the Black man, you stick out your chest and say, "See, we're solving the problem."

You're not doing the Black man any favor. If you stick a knife in my back, if you put it in nine inches and pull it out six inches, you haven't done me any favor. If you pull it all the way out, you haven't done me any favor. And this is what you have to realize. If you put a man in jail against his will—illegally, he's not guilty—you frame him up, and then because he resents what you've done to him, you put him in solitary confinement to break his spirit, then after his spirit is broken, you let him out a little bit and give him the general run of the prison, you haven't done him any favor. If you let him out of prison completely, you haven't done him any favor, because you put him in there unjustly and illegally in the first place.

Now you have 20 million Black people in this country who were brought here and put in a political, economic, and mental prison. This was done by Uncle Sam. And today you don't realize what a crime your forefathers have committed. And you think that when you open the door a few cracks, and give this little integration-intoxicated Negro a chance to run around in the prison yard— that's all he's doing—that you're doing him a favor. But as long as he has to look up to someone who doesn't represent him and doesn't speak for him, that person only represents the warden, he doesn't represent some kind of

president or mayor or governor or senator or congress-
man or anything else.

So this new type—the fact has to be faced that he
exists. Especially since he's in the house. And he didn't
come here because it was his will. So you have to take the
blame for his being here. And once you take the blame,
then its more easy. Its easier for you to approach the
problem more sensibly and try and get a solution. And the
solution can never be based upon hypocrisy. The Honorable Elijah Muhammad says that this solution has to be
based upon reality. Tokenism is hypocrisy. One little
student in the University of Mississippi, that's hypocrisy.
A handful of students in Little Rock, Arkansas, is hypocrisy.* A couple of students going to school in Georgia is
hypocrisy.

---

* In September 1957, a court-ordered plan to begin desegregation of
the schools in Little Rock, Arkansas, was stymied by Gov. Orval
Faubus, who was seeking a third term of office. The governor posted
members of the Arkansas National Guard outside Central High
School, ostensibly to prevent violence and preserve order. A federal
court ordered the guardsmen to quit the school, and nine Black
students entered the all-white school. When a crowd of angry whites
threatened to lynch the students, city officials ordered the Blacks out.

Reluctantly, President Eisenhower dispatched troops to the site and
placed the national guardsmen under federal command. The Black
students re-entered the school, protected by soldiers, some of whom
remained at Central High until the end of the school year.

Faubus was re-elected. In September 1958 he closed all four of Little
Rock's public high schools. Not until the fall of 1959 did the desegregation process begin to revive.

James Meredith, a Black resident of Mississippi, had been refused
admittance into that state's all-white university in February 1961.
Despite a federal court of appeals ruling and an order by a U.S.
Supreme Court justice that Meredith be allowed to enroll, Gov. Ross
Barnett and state officials blocked his admission. On September 30,
1962, President Kennedy was forced to mobilize more than three
hundred federal marshals to get Meredith into the university. Thousands of troops had to be sent in over the next two days to maintain
order when white vigilantes attacked the marshals. Some three hundred troops were stationed at the university for nearly a year to
prevent further incidents.

Integration in America is hypocrisy in the rawest form. And the whole world can see it. All this little tokenism that is dangled in front of the Negro and then he's told, "See what we're doing for you, Tom." Why the whole world can see that this is nothing but hypocrisy. All you do is make your image worse; you don't make it better.

So again, this new type, as I say, he rejects the white man's Christian religion. You find in large numbers they're turning toward the religion of Islam. They are becoming Muslims, believing in one God, whose proper name is Allah, in Muhammad as his apostle, in turning toward Mecca, praying five times a day, fasting during Ramadan, and all the other principles that are laid out by the religion of Islam. He's becoming a Muslim and just as—I think it was Dr. Billy Graham who made a crusade through Africa and came back and said that Islam is sweeping through Africa, outnumbering Christianity in converts eleven to one, which means every time one African becomes a Christian, eleven of them become a Muslim. And then that one who became a Christian, he forgets it and goes on and be a Muslim, too. [*Laughter*]

So that—and Bishop Pike pointed out the same thing in *Look* magazine in December 1960 and then *Time* magazine, heaven forbid that I should mention that magazine, [*Laughter and applause*] but *Time* magazine mentioned it, two weeks ago, that Islam is sweeping throughout Africa. And just as it is sweeping throughout the Black people of Africa, it is sweeping throughout the Black people right here in America. Only the one who's teaching it here in America is the Honorable Elijah Muhammad. He is the religious leader, the religious teacher. He is the one who is spreading the religion of Islam among the slaves, ex-slaves, here in America.

You have Muslims who have come to this country from the Muslim world. There are probably 200,000 Muslims in this country from the Muslim world, who were born in the Muslim world. And all of them combined have never been able to convert a hundred Americans to the religion of Islam. Yet it is the nature of Islam to propagate the faith, to spread the faith, to make everyone bear witness that there's no God but Allah and Muhammad is his apostle.

And if you find all of the Muslims of the Muslim world who come here, unable or incapable of turning the American people toward Allah and toward Mecca and toward Islam, and then this little Black man from the cotton fields of Georgia is able to stand up and get Black people by the hundreds of thousands to turn toward Mecca five times a day and give praise to Allah and come together in unity and harmony, why you'd have to be out of your mind to think the people of the Muslim world don't recognize the wonderful religious and spiritual accomplishment that's being achieved here among the so-called Negroes by the Honorable Elijah Muhammad.

And I take time to mention that because the propagandists try and convey the picture that we're not Muslims, we're not religiously motivated, and that we are in no way identified or recognized or connected with our people of the Muslim world. Well if they didn't recognize us, we wouldn't care. We're not particularly looking for recognition. We're looking for recognition from Allah, from God, and if Allah accepts you as a Muslim, you're accepted. It's not left to somebody walking around here on this earth. But those people over there would be out of their minds, when they find themselves unable to spread the religion of Islam and then they see this little Black man here in America spreading it, why they'd be out of their mind to reject him. And you'll find if you take the time to look, that you don't find any Muslim today who rejects another Muslim.

You might find some who come over here, who operate stores or some kind of little business in the white neighborhood, the Christian neighborhood, and they want to get along with all the white people, with all the Christians. They might say some words to please you. But they're only trying to get your money.

So the followers of the Honorable Elijah Muhammad look to him and what he teaches, his program and his message, as our only solution. And they see separation as our only salvation.

We don't think as Americans any more, but as a Black man. With the mind of a Black man, we look beyond America. And we look beyond the interests of the white man. The thinking of this new type of Negro is broad. It's more international. This integrationist always thinks in terms of an American. But you find the masses of Black people today think in terms of Black. And this Black thinking enables them to see beyond the confines of America. And they look all over the world. They look at the happenings in the international context.

By this little integrationist Negro thinking locally, by his thinking and desires being confined to America, he's limited. He's the underdog. He's a minority. But the masses of Black people who have been exposed to the teachings of the Honorable Elijah Muhammad, their thinking is more international. They look on this earth and they see that the majority of the people on this earth are dark. And by seeing that the majority of the people on this earth are dark, they don't regard themselves as a minority in America, but rather they regard themselves as part of that vast, dark majority.

So therefore, when you run into that type of Black man, he doesn't speak as an underdog. He doesn't speak like you outnumber him, or he doesn't speak like there's any harm that you can do to him. He speaks as one who outnumbers you. He sees that the dark world outnumbers the white world. That the odds have turned today and are in his favor, are on his side. He sees that the people of this earth are on his side. That time is on his side. That history is on his side. And most important of all, he sees that God is on his side toward getting him some kind of solution that's immediate, and that's lasting, and that is no way connected or concerned or stems from the goodwill or good conscience in any way, shape, 'soever of the man who created—who committed the crime and created the problem in the first place.

I would like to point out, quickly and briefly—no I won't, I think my time is up.

Voice: Just about.

Well Dr. here says my time is up, and I'm telling him his time is short. [*Laughter*] So I think what's good for the goose is good for the gander.

DISCUSSION PERIOD

[*Following an extended comment by someone in the audience, there were questions from the floor.*]

Question: Do you consider Elijah Muhammad as a prophet or as a leader?

Malcolm X: We never refer to the Honorable Elijah Muhammad as a prophet. He never refers to himself as that, and he teaches us that the world has no need for prophets today. But he's a leader, he's a leader of the Black people here in this country against the oppression and exploitation that our people have suffered for 400 years. And we need a leader from among ourselves, because our people back home never came and tried to relieve us of the suffering that we've undergone.

Question: I'm a white man—

Malcolm X: You're not a white man.

Question: If I was a white man, do you accept him to attend your mosque, to worship God with you?

Malcolm X: If the—all of the Muslims in this country from Egypt and elsewhere have not been successful in getting the white man to turn toward the religion of Islam and they are born in the Muslim world, well we find we'd be wasting our time trying to convert the white man ourself. Mr. Muhammad is primarily concerned with the condition of the Black man in this country.

Now if the other Muslims who come here from abroad

want to set up some kind of mosque and let the white man in it and teach him how to be a Muslim and get him to say, "No God but Allah," then they can do that. But they shouldn't criticize us for not doing it, because they haven't succeeded in doing it.

Question: Will you accept me in your mosque?

Malcolm X: Sir, you're not white.

Question: I'm asking you if a white man, many people are white men and they are Muslim too.

Malcolm X: I answered you. Mr. Muhammad's concern is not with the white man. His concern is with the Black man. . . . Islam means to submit to the will of one God whose personal and proper name is Allah. What you forget, if you're in the Muslim world practicing Islam, you're not faced with the same problem of Black people who have been kidnapped from the Muslim world and have been deprived of Islam.

[*Question unintelligible*]

Malcolm X: You have to ask the white man that. He's the one who segregates us. Segregation is done by him. You have to ask him that question. . . . Sir, I just want to add some light to your question.

We are brothers. Mr. Muhammad's youngest son attends al-Azhar, and his brother-in-law, in Egypt too. We are brothers, I was in Egypt. I lived in Egypt, I stayed in Egypt, and I was among brothers and I felt the spirit of brotherhood. But an Egyptian who comes to America should realize the problem confronted by Black people in this country. And when you see us being chased by a dog, the best thing for you to do is wait until the dog stops chasing us and then ask us some questions. Especially when you should have come a long time ago and helped your little brothers whip the dog. [*Applause*]

[*Question unintelligible*]

Malcolm X: There are many different ways to understand politics. Number one, we're not a political group. We are not politically inclined or motivated nor are our political aims in any way connected with the Honorable Elijah Muhammad. But when you study the science of politics, or study it as it's practiced in the UN at the international level, you'll find usually on questions you have those who say yes, those who say no, those who don't say anything.

Those who don't say anything usually are the neutrals. And by abstaining they have just as much political power, if not more so, than those who take an active part in all situations. Where the Negro in America is concerned, he's been without the ballot so long, today when he gets the ballot, he's ballot-happy. He's like the man to whom you give a gun, and he just starts shooting to let everybody know he's got a gun. He doesn't aim at anything.

Well, we believe in shooting, too. But we first believe that we should have a target and then when that target gets within our reach, then we'll put the bullet where it belongs. Or the ballot where it belongs. Whatever you call it, where it belongs. We don't see at this point where the Black man gains anything in politics.

Let me just give you an example. In the last presidential election, whites were evenly divided between Kennedy and Nixon. It was the Negro who went for Kennedy, 80 percent, and put Kennedy in the White House. And they went for him based upon the promises—false promises, by the way—that he made. Well, facts are facts. He said he [*Applause*]—I think everybody has a right to his opinion. [*Laughter*] And I'm quite certain those who are familiar with Kennedy's promises to the Negro know what he said he could do with the stroke of his pen. And he was in office for two years before he found where his fountain pen was [*Laughter and applause*] where the Negro was concerned. [*Applause*]

And the excuse that he used was that he first had to change the attitude of southern segregationists. Now he didn't tell you that when he asked you to vote for him. But once he got in, then he had to tell you what problems he was facing. He didn't want to take a stand against the southern segregationists. But he did take a stand against U.S. Steel, which is the strongest corporation on this earth. He threw down the gauntlet. He threw down the gauntlet to Cuba. He has thrown down the gauntlet to anybody he desires. But when it comes to the Negro, he's always got an alibi that puts him off until a little while later. This is why we don't believe in any white politicians or anything like that can solve our problem. We'll get together among ourselves, with these students who go to these colleges and get equipped and solve the problem for ourselves. . . .

[Question unintelligible]

Malcolm X: Whenever you send 15,000 troops and spend six or seven million dollars just to put one Negro in the midst of some yapping wolves, you haven't done that Negro nor the masses of Black people any favor, nor have you solved the problem. If it's legal and just and right for Meredith to be at the University of Mississippi according to Robert Kennedy, the attorney general, and all of the others, then every other Black man in Mississippi has just as much right to be there. So if you're going to spend all that money and all that manpower putting one in there, why not just go in and take the criminals who are responsible for keeping the masses out, and take them down off their posts and then open the doors to everybody. That would be a solution, but they're not going to do that. They always want to use methods that push one Negro at a time, then they use him to turn around and tell the masses, "You see, we're solving the problem." And the problem is still unsolved. . . .

The Honorable Elijah Muhammad says the only way to solve the problem of the so-called Negro is complete separation in the United States. . . . The Honorable Elijah Muhammad says, every effort on the part of the government up till now to solve this problem by bringing about a just, equitable situation between whites and

Blacks mixed up together here in this house has failed. Has failed absolutely. So he says that since you can't give the Negro justice in your house, let us leave this house and go back home.

Now at the same time that he says let us go back home to our own people and our own homeland, the government itself is the leading opposer toward any mass element of Black people becoming orientated in the direction of home. They put forth the effort to stop this. So what he says is, since you can't give it to us here mixed up in your house, and you don't want us to go home back to our own people, then the only alternative is to separate the house. Give us part of this country and let us live in that part. [*Laughter*]

You've asked me to explain. Now you want me to proceed? You may think its funny, but one of these days you won't. [*Applause*] . . . He says that in this section that will be set aside for Black people, that the government should give us everything we need to start our own civilization. They should give us everything we need to exist for the next twenty-five years. And when you stop and consider the—you shouldn't be shocked, you give Latin America $20 billion and they never fought for this country. They never worked for this country. You send billions of dollars to Poland and to Hungary, they're Communist countries, they never contributed anything here. [*Applause*]

This is what you should realize. The greatest contribution to this country was that which was contributed by the Black man. If I take the wages, just a moment, if I take the wages of everyone here, individually it means nothing, but collectively all of the earning power or wages that you earned in one week would make me wealthy. And if I could collect it for a year, I'd be rich beyond dreams. Now, when you see this, and then you stop and consider the wages that were kept back from millions of Black people, not for one year but for 310 years, you'll see how this country got so rich so fast. And what made the economy as strong as it is today. And all that, and all of that slave labor that was amassed in unpaid wages, is due someone today. And you're not giving us anything when we say that it's time to collect.

[*Question unintelligible*]

Malcolm X: Up until a few years ago, the whole dark world, which was then the majority, was ruled by Europe—the white man, who was actually a minority.

And realizing that they were only ruled because of the scientific effort put forth to divide and conquer by the European whites, all of the people black, brown, red, and yellow in Africa got together in what was known as the Bandung Conference.* They realized that they had religious differences, economic differences, educational differences, even cultural differences. And they agreed to submerge all of their differences because they had one thing in common—oppression, exploitation. And they had an oppressor in common, an exploiter in common—the European. Once they realized they had this in common, they had a common enemy and they reached the agreement not to fight among themselves anymore.

And just by being able to submerge their own differences and come together in a spirit of unity, the Bandung Conference produced the condition by which all of the nations in Africa that are independent today were able to secure their independence. And so they have come into the UN. Now they are in a position they can outvote the white man. And it has actually created an accomplish-

---

* The Bandung Conference, held in April 1955 in Bandung, Indonesia, was an ideological forerunner of the Movement of Nonaligned Countries. Sponsored by Burma, Indonesia, India, Ceylon (Sri Lanka), and Pakistan, the conference was attended by representatives of twenty-nine countries. Part of its announced goal was "to consider problems of special interest to Asian and African peoples, for example, problems affecting national sovereignty and of racialism and colonialism."

ment. Whereas in the past you had European, white Christians always at the helm in the UN, today the black, brown, red, and yellow people of Africa and Asia so greatly outnumber the white man, they can't get a white, Christian European elected to any position of power. Usually, the secretariat and the president's chair stays in the hands of an African, an Asian, a Muslim, a Hindu, or a Christian. This is what unity is able to do.

And here in America, the Negro, the so-called Negroes, all we have to do is forget our differences. Usually whites cite things to try and divide us, and then use us one against the other. They try and use the NAACP against the Muslims, Muslims against CORE; they try and keep them all fighting one another. And as we fight one another, they continue to rule. So what the Honorable Elijah Muhammad says is what you and I should do is forget all of our differences and put first things first. Get at the one who's holding both of us down and we can talk to each other later on.

[Question unintelligible]

Malcolm X: The South African whites are, number one, on a continent where they don't belong and have no business there and won't be there that much longer. *[Laughter and applause]* The Black people in South Africa outnumber the whites there about eleven to one. *[Applause]* The Blacks in South Africa outnumber the whites. Enough to get rid of them when the time comes. Now, their type of separation is not the type of separation that we're looking for. We're looking for a separation in which we have our own. We can either go back home and practice it or we can stay here and practice it. But we are not going to sit around with this integration hypocrisy that whites are talking about which will take another hundred years. The only thing you can bring about in the morning is complete separation. It has no connection or comparison whatsoever with that which is being practiced in South Africa.

South African apartheid is segregation. It's not separation. And they are afraid to let those Africans build up a society of their own in which they will become equal or just as powerful politically, economically, and otherwise as the whites are in their parts. They don't want that. No, no comparison whatsoever. Theirs is something of the past, it's outmoded and it's on its way out. Ours is riding on the wave of the future. . . .

[*Question unintelligible*]

Malcolm X: If you can't receive justice in a man's house, that man deprives you of justice, he should let you leave. And if he doesn't want you to leave his house, yet he can't give you justice in the house, he'll end up losing the whole house himself. This is what America is faced with.

[*Question unintelligible*]

Malcolm X: No, the Fruit—you asked another question within that—the Fruit of Islam are the brothers who have been reformed, rehabilitated; who don't drink, don't smoke, don't commit fornication or adultery, don't become involved in any kind of crime. Who learn how to respect their women—to respect the Black woman, who has never had any respect or protection in this society. These are the brothers who have actually reformed themselves and they set an example of what the religion of Islam will do for others of the so-called Negroes. And these brothers will give you respect when you respect them.

[*Question unintelligible*]

Malcolm X: No, they don't comprise a small army. But an army in this sense—army only means a lot of people. They don't comprise an army in the sense that they are looking for violence. But you will find this: that a Muslim brother, whenever he's attacked, he'll defend himself.

[*Question unintelligible*]

Malcolm X: No, I'll answer the last question first. No, there's no such thing as a sincere white liberal—listen I'm giving you my answer. You can hiss all night, that's what the snake did in the Garden of Eden. [*Laughter and applause*] Usually you'll find, sir, that in any integrated group that the so-called Negro has, if you examine its composition, where the whites are concerned, they end up leading it, they end up ruling it, they end up controlling it.

I'll give you an example. The NAACP is one of the leading organizations that Negroes have. It has been in existence for fifty-four years, and the Black people in the NAACP have never had enough power in there to elect a Black man as the national president. They have an election every year. Which means they have had an election fifty-four times in fifty-four years. And every time, they've had to elect a white man. The man who is the president of it now, Arthur Spingarn, has been president of it for twenty-four consecutive years.

Now if—I'm not knocking the NAACP—but if the NAACP—I'm just, uhm, analyzing it. [*Laughter*] If the NAACP in fifty-four years cannot get a Black man qualified to be its national president, then it leads me to believe either they are failing to create and develop the proper leadership caliber among the Black people in it, or else they are practicing the same discrimination that they accuse the white man of.

Where CORE is concerned—the Urban League is another famous Negro organization that's integrated. It has a white president. It has never had a Black president. CORE has a Negro national director; but he's a Negro who's married to a white woman. James Farmer, he's married to a white woman and that almost makes him a white man. Although they have a Black—they have a white president also. It's true—Farmer, in 1945, divorced his Black wife and married a white woman.

[*Question unintelligible*]

Malcolm X: In the UN with the Lebanese or Arabs—in the UN you have the Afro-Asian-Arab bloc. Now a lot of Arabs might like for you to think that they are white, but whenever you see them involved in the international picture, they are lined up with the dark world. Those who are making progress are lined up with the dark world. Afro-Asian-Arab. They can come around here and pose as white. But when they get back home, they're not white. . . .

[*Question unintelligible*]

Malcolm X: You never heard me today refer to myself as a Black Muslim. This is what the press says. We call ourselves Muslim. Just a moment. We call ourselves Muslim—we don't call ourselves Black Muslims. This is what the newspapers call us. This is what Dr. Eric Lincoln calls us. We are Muslims. Black, brown, red, and yellow.

[*Question unintelligible*]

Malcolm X: Now you say that we come here and use Islam for political purposes because we reject the white man. When the Algerians refused to integrate with the French, did that make, mean that they weren't Muslims? When the Arabs refused to integrate with the Israelis, does that mean they're not Muslims? When the Pakistanis refused to integrate with the Hindus, does that mean they're not Muslims? No, just a moment. The Algerians have the right to reject the French, who exploited them. The Arabs have the right to reject the Israelis, whom they feel exploit them. The Pakistanis have the right to reject the Hindus, whom they feel exploit them. The Algerians are still Muslims. The Arabs are still Muslims and the Pakistanis are still Muslims. There are 20 million Black people in this country who have been here for 400 years. And who have suffered the worst form of abuse ever perpetrated on a people in the twentieth century. Now when we accept Islam as our religion, that doesn't mean that we are religiously wrong to reject the man who has exploited us and colonized us here in this country.

[*Question unintelligible*]

Malcolm X: It's not wrong to expect justice. It's not

wrong to expect freedom. It's not wrong to expect equality. If Patrick Henry and all of the Founding Fathers of this country were willing to lay down their lives to get what you are enjoying today, then it's time for you to realize that a large, ever-increasing number of Black people in this country are willing to die for what we know is due us by birth.

The white man is being given a favor, when you give him a chance today to solve a problem that stems from a crime that he committed himself. You ask me—like I'm committing a crime or asking for something that's ethically wrong or morally wrong when we seek a solution to this problem right now. A problem that has the government all tied up all over this earth. What you need to realize, you from India, you from Iraq, you from Egypt, and you from right here in America, and we who are enslaved—that a crime has been committed against the Negro. Some of you from over there, you knew we were over here and never come over here to help us, and now when we stand up and are ready to help ourselves, don't come with your criticism. Help us.

[*Question unintelligible*]

Malcolm X: Would you think that I was wrong if I asked: how are you going to integrate? If the Supreme Court says integrate, and they can't do it, and that's the highest court—we're not rejecting anything. We reserve—I said no, he asked me was I rejecting, were we rejecting violence or were we rejecting peaceful methods. We don't reject any methods. We leave—we reserve the right to use whatever method that will bring about a solution to the problem and then when—and the reason that I haven't—Sir, I don't think you would give me credit. If you have a lamb inside of a wolf's den and you need to get that lamb out of the clutches of that wolf, you don't stand up and tell the lamb, how are you going to take him, or where you're going to take him, while he's still in the clutches of the wolf, or while he's still under the jurisdiction of the wolf. . . .

[Question unintelligible]

Malcolm X: As you say, [Uncle] Tom always was a good actor. And where the white man thinks we're dangerous to him, Tom is more dangerous to the white man than anyone, because Tom has him fooled.

The white man knows where we stand; but Tom today is waking up the same as anybody else. Well, you won't get any argument out of me. It is true that many Negroes in prominent positions who have been known Uncle Toms in the past today are waking up, and their allegiances and other aims are very much camouflaged still, as they were then. . . .

[Question unintelligible]

Malcolm X: We'll do it the same way the Jews got what they wanted. They got their own state, their own country. No, they got it, and yeah, well you're right, it was given to them by England and Truman. But, sir, no the Jews are the ones who usually represent themselves as white liberals. More so probably than any other segment of this society. Now if the Jews are genuinely liberal and they want to help the Negro, then they should show the Negro how to use the same kind of strategy and tactics to solve his problem that they used to solve their problems. And you'll find that all over this country, wherever the Jews have been segregated and Jim Crowed, they haven't sat-in, they haven't been sit-in or Freedom Riders, they usually go and use the economic weapon. They bought Atlantic City, and now they can go there. They bought Miami Beach and now they can go there. *[Laughter and applause]*

America's gravest crisis since the Civil War

MR. MODERATOR, students and faculty here at the University of California, brothers and sisters, friends and enemies. [*Laughter*] The bell up there took so long to stop ringing, I began to suspect that it was probably being manipulated by an integrationist. [*Laughter and applause*]

Recently the state of California, the Supreme Court here, denied Negro inmates who had become converted to the religion of Islam while serving time in these penal institutions of this state, denied them the right to receive qualified Muslim religious instructors from the outside on the ground that the Muslims who follow the Honorable Elijah Muhammad are not an authentic religious group.

At the same time, the state's esteemed body of educators here at the University of California barred me from speaking on this campus on the grounds that we do represent an authentic religious group. [*Laughter*] It meant that your top judicial body deprives us of our religious rights by saying we aren't a bona fide religious group, and your top body of educators—I think that's what they'd be called—deprive us of our religious rights by saying we are a bona fide religious group.

Well, I'm happy and thankful to our God, Allah, for enabling them to come to some kind of conclusion as to what we actually are. Because it confused us to see how two important branches of your state government could logically come to opposite conclusions on the same subject.

Or is it that in this state you are permitted the type of intellectual flexibility that enables your state government to speak out of both sides of its mouth in this manner at the same time? And to make certain that there'd be no clarification of the misunderstanding about our religion, I read in the—I think the *San Francisco Chronicle,* or one of your papers, yesterday—that I was permitted to speak here as long as I didn't get into religion, or stuck to what they call secular matters.

So it's not my intention to discuss the Muslim religious group today nor the Muslim religion, but I am a Muslim. But I intend to stick to secular problems. It's like inviting a Catholic priest or bishop here to speak but forbidding him to mention Catholicism or the pope. Or inviting Billy Graham and telling him not to mention Christ. Or a member of the Kennedy family and expecting him not to mention politics.

It boils down to inviting a Muslim minister to speak on what you call secular problems but denying him the right to speak religiously or from a religious point of view. It's like telling a bird to fly without his wings. Or a race horse to run without his legs. Then you condemn that bird that you have crippled yourself and condemn the horse that you've also crippled because it can't keep up. This is very hypocritical. But tomorrow, or Sunday, rather, it's our intention to hold a meeting at the Civic Center in Richmond, at 1:00 p.m. at which time we intend to spell out our religious beliefs, our religious motives, and our religious objectives.

Today during the time that we have, we would like to point out that the Honorable Elijah Muhammad teaches us that America is faced with her gravest crisis since the Civil War. Wherever we look today, whether it be in the South, the North, the East, or the West, we see ever-increasing racial tensions.

We see the increase of racial animosity, the increase of racial hostility, and the increase of outright racial hatred. We see masses of Black people who have lost all confidence in the false promises of the hypocritical white politicians. We see masses of Black people who are thoroughly fed up with the deceit of the so-called white liberals, or the white so-called liberals. White liberals who have posed as our friends, white liberals who have been eager to point out what the white man in the South is doing to our people there, while they themselves are doing the same thing to us here in the North.

They have been making a great fuss over the South only to blind us to what is happening here in the North. And now that the Honorable Elijah Muhammad has opened the eyes of America's 20 million Blacks, we can easily see that this white fox here in the North is even more cruel and more vicious than the white wolf in the South. The southern wolves always let you know where you stand. But these northern foxes pose as white liberals. They pose as your friend, as your benefactor, as your employer, as your landlord, as your neighborhood merchant, as your lawyer. They use integration for infiltration. They infiltrate all your organizations, and in this manner, by joining you, they strangle your militant efforts toward true freedom.

Throughout America, here in the North, as well as the South, masses of Black people are demonstrating against the oppression and exploitation of the American white man. Our people have lost all fear of the white man. They have ceased to waste their love on the white man, and they have ceased turning their nonviolent cheek to the violent white man. And because of this new fearless, more militant attitude on the part of our people, we see the increase of violence and bloodshed between the white oppressor and the oppressed, the white exploiter and the exploited, the white former slavemaster and his 20 million ex-slaves.

The question that is asked, where will all of this end? I repeat, America is faced with her worst domestic crisis since the Civil War. The worst crisis since the Revolutionary War. For America now faces a race war. The entire country is on the verge of erupting into racial violence and bloodshed simply because 20 million ex-slaves here in America are demanding freedom, justice, and equality from their former slavemasters.

Twenty million so-called Negroes, second-class citizens, seeking nothing but human dignity and human rights, the right to live in dignity as a human being. And rather than give genuine sincere respect to your cry for human rights, the American white man answers your nonviolence with violence. He answers your prayers and freedom songs with false promises, deceitful maneuvers, and outright bloodshed.

According to what we were taught from the white man's textbooks in school, the Revolutionary War and the Civil War were two wars fought on American soil supposedly for freedom and democracy. But if these two wars were really fought for freedom and human dignity of all men, why are 20 million of our people still confined and enslaved here in America by second-class citizenship? The truth is that the Revolutionary War was fought on American soil to free the American white man from the English white man. The Revolutionary War was never fought to provide freedom and a democracy in this white country for the Black man. Our people remained slaves here in America even after the Declaration of Independence was signed. In fact most of the white Founding Fathers who signed the Declaration of Independence were slave owners themselves.

The Honorable Elijah Muhammad teaches us that it is sheer ignorance, insanity, for our people to celebrate the Fourth of July as Independence Day, while white America denies us the first-class citizenship that goes with independence. And it is nothing but hypocrisy on the part of the American white man to pretend that the Revolutionary War was truly a war of independence as long as 20 million Black people here in America are denied the privileges of an independent people.

The Civil War was fought on this continent, but not to free the Black slaves as is commonly taught in the white man's schools. The Civil War was actually fought to preserve the Union, to keep the country intact for white people.

The Honorable Elijah Muhammad teaches us that in essence this means the American white man fought the Revolutionary War to get this country for himself. He then fought the Civil War to keep this country intact for himself. And today he will now fight a race war to keep from having to share this country on an equal basis with anyone else but himself. Especially on an equal basis with his 20 million former slaves.

So again I ask, where will these demonstrations end? And who dares to say that our people are not justified in demonstrating our resentment over the injustice and mistreatment that our people have suffered these 400 years at the hands of this cruel, inhuman American white man?

The Black masses are crying out, "What have we to lose but our chains? What have we to lose but the hell that we experience every day living in these rat-filled slums that we're relegated to?" The worst housing conditions in America always exist in the so-called Negro community. Yet the white liberals, who own these run-down houses, force us to pay the highest rent. Faced with this high overhead, we are forced to take in roomers in order to help make up our rent. Our apartments are filled with both relatives and strangers. Our communities soon become overcrowded. These overcrowded conditions under which our people are forced to live eliminate all chances for a normal life, a clean life, or a healthy life.

Because our children grow up in this overcrowded

atmosphere, the lack of much-needed privacy destroys their sense of shame. It lowers their moral standards and leaves them exposed to every form of indecency and vice imaginable. Our young girls, our daughters, our baby sisters become unwed mothers before they are hardly out of their teens. Our community has thousands of unmarried mothers, mothers who have no hope of ever getting a husband. And our community has tens of thousands of little babies who have no father to act as their provider or protector. In fact the only provider many of our children know is the white welfare agent or the white social worker. Many of our children actually mistake the welfare agent or the white social worker for their father. And oftentimes this is true. [*Commotion and applause*]

The overcrowded homes of our community force us to live under some of the worst sanitary conditions imaginable. It becomes almost impossible to practice the rules of good hygiene. And therefore tuberculosis, syphilis, gonorrhea, and other destructive social diseases are on the rampage throughout our community.

Our people in the Negro community are trapped in a vicious cycle of ignorance, poverty, disease, sickness, and death. There seems to be no way out. No way of escape. The wealthy, educated Black bourgeoisie, those uppity Negroes who do escape, never reach back and pull the rest of our people out with them. The Black masses remain trapped in the slums.

And because there seems to be no hope or no other escape, we turn to wine, we turn to whiskey, and we turn to reefers, marijuana, and even to the dreadful needle—heroin, morphine, cocaine, opium—seeking an escape.

Many of us turn to crime, stealing, gambling, prostitution. And some of us are used by the white overlords downtown to push dope in the Negro community among our own people. Unemployment and poverty have forced many of our people into a life of crime. But the real criminal is in the City Hall downtown, in the State

House, and in the White House in Washington, D.C. The real criminal is the white liberal, the political hypocrite. And it is these legal crooks who pose as our friends, force us into a life of crime, and then use us to spread the white man's evil vices in our community among our own people.

The Honorable Elijah Muhammad teaches us that our people are scientifically maneuvered by the white man into a life of poverty. Because we are forced to live in the poorest sections of the city, we attend inferior schools. We have inferior teachers and we get an inferior education. The white power structure downtown makes certain that by the time our people do graduate, we won't be equipped or qualified for anything but the dirtiest, heaviest, poorest-paying jobs. Jobs that no one else wants.

We are trapped in a vicious cycle of economic, intellectual, social, and political death. Inferior jobs, inferior housing, inferior education which in turn again leads to inferior jobs. We spend a lifetime in this vicious circle. Or in this vicious cycle going in circles. Giving birth to children who see no hope or future but to follow in our miserable footsteps.

So we thank God for the Honorable Elijah Muhammad. We who are Muslims saw no way out until we accepted the religion of Islam and the spiritual guidance of the Honorable Elijah Muhammad. We saw no solution to our problems. We saw no real leader among our people.

But today the whole world is talking about the Honorable Elijah Muhammad and the divine solution he received from the God of our forefathers. Not your God but from the God of our forefathers. Not a temporary solution which will benefit only the handpicked upper-class Negroes, but a solution divinely designed to solve the plight of the Black masses in this country permanently and forever.

The government does not want our people to listen and understand the solution that God has given the Honorable Elijah Muhammad. The government is against Mr.

Muhammad because the government is against our God. In order to trick our people away from God's true solutions, the government is trying to deceive our people with a false solution, a phony solution, a deceitful solution called token integration. I may add, whenever you get on the bus or the subway or the streetcar and you have to use a token, that token is not the real thing but it is a substitute for the real thing. And wherever you have a token, you have a substitute. And wherever you have token integration, you don't have anything but a substitute for integration and there's no real integration anywhere in North America—North, South, East, or West, not even in San Francisco, Oakland, or Berkeley. [*Applause*]

Has the government effort to bribe our people with token integration made our plight better, or has it made it worse? When you tried to integrate the white community in search of better housing, the whites there fled to the suburbs. And the community that you thought would be integrated soon deteriorated into another all-Black slum. What happened to the liberal whites? Why did they flee? We thought that they were supposed to be our friends. And why did the neighborhood deteriorate only after our people moved in?

It is the tricky real estate agents posing as white liberal friends who encourage our people to force their way into white communities, and then they themselves sell these integrated houses at such high prices that our people again are forced to take in roomers to offset the high house notes. This creates in the new area the same overcrowded conditions, and the new community soon deteriorates into the same slum conditions from which we thought we had escaped. The only one who has benefited is the white real estate agent who poses as our friend, as a liberal, and who sells us the house in a community destined by his own greedy schemes to become nothing but a high-priced slum area.

Today our people can see that integrated housing has not solved our problems. At best it was only a temporary solution. One in which only the wealthy, handpicked Negroes found temporary benefit.

After the 1954 Supreme Court desegregation decision, the same thing happened when our people tried to integrate the schools. All the white students disappeared into the suburbs. Now the caliber of what our people thought was to be an integrated school has fallen to the same level of the slum school from which we thought we had escaped. Just as efforts to integrate housing failed miserably, efforts to integrate schools have been an even more miserable failure.

Having failed to get integrated housing and failed to get integrated schools, now the Negro leaders are demanding integrated jobs. That is they are demanding a certain quota, or percentage, of white people's jobs.

First the Negro leadership demanded the white man's house, and the whites vacated their run-down houses for us and built new homes for themselves out in the suburbs. Then the Negro leaders demanded seats for our children in the white man's schools. The whites evacuated the schools as our children moved in and they built modern schools for themselves in the suburbs. But now the Negro leadership is demanding the white man's job. Can the whites vacate their jobs like they did their homes and their schools and move to the suburbs and create more jobs? No. Not without violence and bloodshed. The same white liberals who used to praise our people for their patient nonviolent approach have now become openly impatient and violent themselves in defense of their own jobs. Not only in the South but also in the North. Even here in the Bay Area.

For thirty-three years the Honorable Elijah Muhammad has been warning us that the time would come when the white man would not have enough jobs for himself much less enough jobs for our people. So the present demand of our people for more of the white man's jobs must lead to violence and bloodshed. It may even lead to a race war—a bloody race war. And it is the government itself that is now pressing the people of this country into a racial bloodbath.

But the white man is misjudging the times and he is underestimating the American so-called Negro because we're living in a new day. Our people are now a new people. That old Uncle Tom–type Negro is dead. Our people have no more fear of anyone, no more fear of anything. We are not afraid to go to jail. We are not afraid to give our very life itself. And we're not afraid to take the lives of those who try to take our lives. We believe in a fair exchange. [*Applause*]

We believe in a fair exchange. An eye for an eye. A tooth for a tooth. A head for a head and life for a life. If this is the price of freedom, we won't hesitate to pay the price. [*Applause*]

By trying to oppose the divine solution that God has given to the Honorable Elijah Muhammad, the American government will actually provoke another Civil War. That is, this government—and especially that present administration in Washington, D.C.—will provoke a civil war among whites by trying to force them to give up their jobs and homes and schools to our people. And our people will provoke a race war by trying to take the white man's jobs and his schools and his home away from him.

This racial dilemma poses a serious problem for white America. Civil war between whites on the one hand, a race war between the whites and their 20 million ex-slaves on the other hand. And the entire dark world is watching, waiting to see what the American government will do to solve this problem once and for all.

We must have a permanent solution. A temporary solution won't do. Tokenism will no longer suffice. The Honorable Elijah Muhammad has the only permanent solution. Twenty million ex-slaves must be permanently separated from our former slavemaster and placed on some land that we can call our own. Then we can create our own jobs. Control our own economy. Solve our own problems instead of waiting on the American white man to solve our problems for us.

The Honorable Elijah Muhammad teaches us that on our own land we can set up farms, factories, businesses. We can establish our own government and become an independent nation. And once we become separated from the jurisdiction of this white nation, we can then enter into trade and commerce for ourselves with other independent nations. This is the only solution.

The Honorable Elijah Muhammad says that in our own land we can establish our own agricultural system. We can grow food to feed our own people. We can raise cattle and use the hides, the leather, and the wool to clothe our people. We can dig the clay from the earth and make bricks to build homes for our people. We can turn the trees into lumber and furnish the homes for our own people.

He says that we can dig the natural resources from the earth once we are in our own land. Land is the basis of all economic security. Land is essential to freedom, justice, and equality. Land is essential to true independence. And the Honorable Elijah Muhammad says we must be separated from the American white man, returned to our own land where we can live among our own people. This is the only true solution.

For just as the biblical government of Egypt under Pharaoh was against Moses because Moses had been directed by God to separate the Hebrew slaves from Pharaoh and lead them out of the house of bondage to a land of their own, today this modern house of bondage under the authority of the American government opposes this modern Moses. Opposes the Honorable Elijah Muhammad's efforts to separate our people, who have been made slaves here in this country, and lead us to a land of our own.

The government opposes the Honorable Elijah Muhammad's efforts to wake us up, clean us up, and stand us on our own feet so we can follow him out of this house of bondage to our own land where we can live among our own people. Just as the government of biblical Egypt was against the God of the Hebrew slaves, today the American government is against the God of her Negro slaves, the God of our forefathers. And just as that Pharaoh tried to trick the Hebrew slaves into rejecting the offers of salvation from their God by deceiving them with false promises through hired magicians and carefully staged demonstrations like the recent ridiculous march on Washington,* today this government is paying certain elements of the Negro leadership to deceive our people into thinking that we're going to get accepted soon into the mainstream of American life.

The government is deceiving our people with false promises so we won't want to return to our own land and people. The government is saying, "Stay here, don't listen to this Muhammad, we will desegregate the lunch counters and the theaters and the parks and the toilets"— meaning this public accommodation thing where you can sit on a toilet with a white person or in a toilet with a white person. [*Applause*]

"We'll give you more civil rights bills. We won't give you civil rights, but we'll give you civil rights bills." The government promises our people this only to keep you from listening to the Honorable Elijah Muhammad and to stop us from waking up. They know that if we listen to the Honorable Elijah Muhammad long enough, we will begin to do our own thinking. He'll make us see, hear, think, and able to speak for ourselves.

---

* The 1963 civil rights march drew more than 250,000 people for an August 28 rally at the Lincoln Memorial. The dominant theme of the march was the call for passage of civil rights legislation then pending in Congress.

Whenever you become fed up in this country with the white man's brutality and you get set to take matters in your own hands in order to defend yourself and your people, the same government—and again I repeat, especially that Catholic administration in Washington, D.C.—tries to pacify our people with deceitful promises of tricky civil rights legislation that is never designed to be a true solution to our problem. Civil rights legislation will never solve our problems. The white liberals are nothing but political hypocrites who use our people as political footballs only to get bills passed that will increase their own power.

The present proposed civil rights legislation will give the present administration dictatorial powers and make America a legal police state, but still won't solve the race problem. The present administration is only using civil rights as a political football to gain more legislation and power for itself. Our people are being used as pawns in the game of power politics by political hypocrites. They don't want our people to listen to the Honorable Elijah Muhammad because they know he will make them—make us see them as they really are.

So I say in my conclusion, the Honorable Elijah Muhammad's message and solution is simple. He says: "Since we are not wanted in this country, let's pack our bags and go back home to our own people, to our own land." The propaganda of the American government is skillfully designed to make our people think that our people back home don't want us. Government propagandists tell us constantly, "Africa is a jungle. Africans are savage and backward. They have no modern conveniences and you're too much like us white folks. How could you live comfortably back there?"

This propaganda is government strategy against the Honorable Elijah Muhammad, realizing that his mission is to teach our people the truth about our own kind, clean us up, and then return us to our own land and unite us with our own people. The American government turns us against our own kind in order to keep us from making a mass exodus out of this country where we can live at home among our own people.

Therefore, the Honorable Elijah Muhammad says, American propaganda is designed to make us think that no matter how much hell we catch here, we're still better off in America than we'd be anywhere else. They want us to think we have no place else to go. And many of our so-called intellectuals who pose as our leaders and spokesmen actually believe that we have no place else to go. So their solution to our problem is that we stay here and continue to catch hell from the American white man.

But the only permanent solution is complete separation or some land of our own in a country of our own. All other courses will lead to violence and bloodshed. It will lead to the destruction of America, and it will also lead to the destruction of our people who fall for it. So his message is flee for your lives and save yourselves. And I thank you. [*Applause*]

DISCUSSION PERIOD

Question: In the last issue of *Muhammad Speaks* there was an article telling of the elimination of racial discrimination in Cuba; telling how Afro- and Latin-Cubans lived in harmony. How does this jibe with the devil concept of the white man and that the idea that freedom can only be achieved through separation? [*Applause*]

Malcolm X: The Cubans don't refer to themselves either as white people or Black people. They refer to themselves as people. You find the American white man is the one who has laid such stress on being white or being black. When you become a Muslim, you don't look at a man as being black, brown, red, or yellow. You look upon him as being a man. And this is something that is foreign to the American concept.

I don't know anything about Cuba. The article was written by Howard, a UN correspondent who spent time in Cuba along with the son of the Honorable Elijah Muhammad when all of the students went. And they did say that they found a great deal of equality, freedom, and justice among the people of Cuba. So I think that in that direction Castro has made a great accomplishment and contribution, but I haven't been there myself.

Now, when you try and bring the same thing about between the American white man and the American Black man, you're dealing with a man who used to have as total possession over the Black people in this country as a farmer has possession over his cow, his chickens, his horse. And this has created an attitude among American whites that they themselves find almost impossible to eliminate. And unless it is eliminated and until it is eliminated the problem will get worse instead of better. I personally don't think it will ever be eliminated. . . .

Question: How do you intend to gain possession of this land that you want and how do you intend to get there?

Malcolm X: That's a good question. Number one, we didn't have any trouble getting to America because the white man—[*Laughter and applause*] By that I mean we weren't Pilgrims. We didn't come on the *Mayflower,* and we didn't come from Europe, and we didn't come of our own volition. We were brought here in chains at the bottom of a slave ship. And since we didn't pay transportation here, the Honorable Elijah Muhammad says that the contribution that the Black man made in this country, which amounts to 310 years of slave labor for which we have never been given a dime or a cent, places a burden upon the American white man today for which the government should pay. And he says that our people should be allowed to go back to our own homeland, that the government itself should supply us with the transportation.

And that they should supply us with the machinery and the tools necessary that will enable us to dig the soil and develop our own agricultural system and feed ourselves for the next twenty to twenty-five years until we are in a position to be completely independent and stand on our own feet. And he says that if the government does not want a mass exodus of Black people from this country back to our own homeland, since we cannot live in peace, together, mixed up on this continent, the alternative to that solution is to divide a separate part of this country into which our people can migrate.

For your clarification, because this has been brought up, some people say, "Well, why should the government do this?" If this government can send billions of dollars to Communist countries like Poland and Yugoslavia and to neutralist countries in Asia and Africa, who have never made any contribution whatsoever to the sum, net worth of this economy and country, and at the same time, this government feels that it is too much to set about something real to solve the problem for the slaves who made a greater contribution than even your people did, why the government doesn't even deserve to continue to function as a government. [*Applause*]

Question: You mentioned again, just now, land set aside for your people, sir. What land is available that's not already possessed by others?

Malcolm X: When you came to this country the land was inhabited by the Indians and you didn't have any problem then. [*Applause*]

Question: Actually, I have two questions. The first one I would like to ask you: Do you believe in Islam just because it gives you dignity as a Black man living in America? Or do you believe in Islam as a whole? So, if you believe in Islam as a whole, you know that Islam believes in socialism rather than capitalism. This is the first question. The second question: You said that Muhammad taught you that you should have your own land so you can find all, to do what you want in it. Will you please give me one statement either from the Koran or from Muhammad's speeches which says, you know, asks for this situation. [*Applause*]

Malcolm X: If I understood my Muslim brother correctly, I hope that he's aware of the fact that my opening statement pointed out that the front page of the *San Francisco Chronicle,* I think it was, told me that the only way I could come here and speak was to speak on secular matters rather than religious, and for that reason I pointed out at the outset that I wasn't going to get onto the religion of Islam. Since you, as a student I imagine, brought it up, it does open the door for me to reply and I thank you for it. [*Applause*]

Number one, Islam is a word which means in Arabic complete submission to the will of God. Complete obedience to the will of God. And this means—and the Jews referred to this God as Jehovah. They're monotheistic. The Christians referred to him, I think, as Christ. Only they're polytheistic, and it's difficult to give one name to their many gods. [*Applause*]

So that in Islam, since we believe that there is one God, we believe that all of the prophets who came forth on this earth taught the same religion. Abraham was a Muslim; Moses was a Muslim; Jesus was a Muslim. And as Black men in America, we accept the religion of Islam because we recognize it as the true religion of God. This is why I'm a Muslim. I am a Muslim because the Honorable Elijah Muhammad has taught me that Islam is God's only religion. And it does say in the Holy Koran that this religion will overcome all other religions.

We believe that we're living in the day and the time and at the hour when God intends to make this religion, Islam, overcome all other religions. This is why we're Muslims. And we want to separate ourselves from America, because we believe that when God comes to establish the religion of Islam or the kingdom of Islam or the world of Islam, he can't do so without first destroying all other religions, governments, nations, and worlds that stand in his way. All governments that won't accept one religion and practice the principles of brotherhood, freedom, justice, and equality among all people, regardless of color, regardless of race or anything else involved, we believe that they'll be destroyed today, and we don't think that you can get the American people to accept the religion of Islam. I have no knowledge of socialism. That's something else. [*Applause*]

Question: Sir, you seem to interchange the term white liberal with hypocritical politician. I don't believe this is true. I don't believe that our white liberals are in office. They are, by the way, investigating—

Moderator: Do you have a question please?

Question: I just wondered why you interchanged these terms when they're so evidently not interchangeable.

Malcolm X: Historically in America, the white liberal has been the one always supposedly who has the solution to the race problem. An example: the leading white liberal in American history was supposed to be Abraham Lincoln. He's the one who has been dangled in front of our people as a god who brought us out of slavery into the promised land of freedom. Martin Luther King last year was begging President Kennedy to issue another Emancipation Proclamation. If the Emancipation Proclamation of Abraham Lincoln was authentic and produced the results that it was supposed to and if it had been sincere, it would have gotten results. Then Martin Luther King wouldn't have to be begging for another proclamation of emancipation today.

And other times—the white liberals supposedly fought the Civil War to free the slaves, and our people are still slaves, still begging for freedom. Some more white liberals came along with the so-called Thirteenth, Fourteenth, Fifteenth, and other amendments to the Constitution supposedly to solve our problem. The Constitution has been amended and the problem is still here.

Nine white liberals on the Supreme Court bench came up with a desegregation decision in 1954 supposedly to desegregate the schools, and the schools haven't been desegregated yet. Kennedy ran on a platform as a white liberal three years ago and said all he had to do was take out his fountain pen and put his name on some paper and our problem would be solved, and it was three years in office before he found where his fountain pen was, and the problem isn't solved yet. [*Laughter and applause*]

Question: I'm a second-generation American, and my people came over in the bottom of ships. And they had second-class citizenship in Europe, and they lived in ghettos and things of this sort, and they got out of them. How come I have attitudes toward Negroes that may be prejudiced? Where did I get these attitudes, if they weren't from the Negro people? None of my people ever owned slaves, or anything of this sort. How did I get my prejudices?

Malcolm X: If you didn't steal the property, you can be held responsible today for being in possession of stolen goods. The book says that the sins of the fathers will be visited upon the heads of the children even unto the seventh generation. And although there are many whites who came here from Europe after 1865, they fit right into the whole, overall pattern of exploitation, of modern slavery, that still exists in this country today. Because it's only a modern form of slavery that our people experience today, and white liberals, again, encourage us to join groups that they set up that they call the National Advance—National Association for the Advancement of Some Colored People, from ancient slavery to modern slavery. [*Commotion and applause*]

If I may add, your mention of white immigrants just coming here proves the inability of Negroes to solve this problem by the present course, or the past course that they've been taking. It's true, Italians, French, Spanish, and others came here as immigrants, uneducated, poverty-stricken. And their parents were able to open up stores. Little stores. They lived in the back, sent their children to school. Their children studied business and came back and expanded the businesses, and most businesses in the white community are called so-and-so brothers, so-and-so and son, and so forth. This is how you established what you call the American economy, somewhat—speaking on the run.

Negroes have been here, free, since 1865, so-called, have a purchasing power of $20 billion per year, have more education than any group, any minority group on this earth. You can't go in the Negro community anywhere in the Bay Area and find five businesses owned by Negroes, so-and-so and son or so-and-so brothers.

The mistake that we made differs from the mistake you didn't make. Your parents solved your problems economically, of their own volition, with their own ingenuity. Our leaders have done nothing to teach us how to go in business. They have done nothing to teach us how to elevate the level of our schools. They've done nothing to teach us how to keep up the standard of our community.

It is not some masses of Black people who are at fault for this. It's this Negro puppet that the white liberal has set over the Negro community to act as our leader and act as our spokesman who has failed to show us how to solve our own problems. So we remain crippled, and accept to follow the advice of this white liberal who does nothing but continue to exploit us instead of trying to help us solve the problem.

Hope I didn't answer you too long.

Moderator: We have time for only one more question, I'm afraid, and I recognize this gentleman.

Question: I'd like to ask Mr. X simply, why cannot a Negro infiltrate the political machine and use power politics to his own end?

Malcolm X: If he studies the science of politics, he probably would. Most Negroes don't. They become involved politically from an emotional point of view rather than a scientific point of view. You show me a Negro politician, and I'll show you one who's controlled by the white political machine. And if you show me one who isn't controlled by the white political machine, I'll show you one whom the white political machine has labeled as a racist, an extremist.

Adam Powell is one of the best examples of it. Anyone that they endorse, who will do what they want him to do, he's all right. But when you become politically independent in this country, the white media, they label you as a racist. The reason for this is, the only way you can become politically independent of the white political machine is to have the support of the Black masses. The only way you can get the support of the Black masses is to say how they think and how they feel. And when you begin to speak to the Black masses, how they feel and think, then the whites call you a racist. Because you have to talk in the context of the intense degree of dissatisfaction that exists in the Negro community.

Whites don't want to hear this. They want to be told that the problem is being solved. You're not solving the problem for anybody but a few handpicked, Uncle Tom Negroes who benefit from your token integration. And as long as you deal with that, you're going to be adding more powder to a keg that's inside your house that can blow you higher, that could explode, higher than a million-megaton bomb. So when you go down here and find how the masses of Black people really feel, you're too intelligent to act as you are, if you know how they really feel. And the only Black man who will tell you exactly how a Black man feels is the Honorable Elijah Muhammad. The rest of them are going to talk to you out of the corner of their mouth. Try and make friends with you.

PART 2

Two December 1964 interviews

After it became clear, in early 1964, that Elijah Muhammad would not ungag Malcolm X, he left the Nation of Islam. In April, he made a pilgrimage to Mecca and a trip to Africa. He returned to the U.S. in May. In the fall, he again visited the Middle East and Africa. These trips had a profound effect on him.

On December 27, he was interviewed on Les Crane's talk show to be aired the following day. At first, Malcolm appeared reluctant to discuss what had caused the rift between himself and his former mentor. But when Les Crane pressed him, he replied, "There were things that happened between me and Elijah Muhammad that caused me to greatly question his ability as a man, much less as a religious leader."

Malcolm frankly acknowledged that many of the things he had said as Elijah Muhammad's spokesman had not been his own views: "Whenever I opened my mouth, I always said that Elijah Muha—the Honorable Elijah Muhammad—teaches us thus and so. And I spoke for him. I represented him. . . . Many of my own views . . . I kept to myself."

On the Bernice Bass show, Malcolm again acknowledged that, as Mr. Muhammad's spokesman, he had merely been parroting Elijah's views. But he pointedly added, "The parrot has jumped out of the cage."

Returning from trip
to Mecca, Saudi
Arabia, and Africa,
May 1964. *(Photo:
Robert Haggins)*

Whatever is necessary to protect ourselves

LES CRANE: My next guest is Mr. Malcolm X, ladies and gentleman. [*Applause*]
This interview is going to be a little difficult for me to do, because I know Malcolm. We've done shows together before. He's been a guest of mine on a couple of different occasions. We've had telephone conversations of length and interest. And—so to get the story, I'm going to make believe that we've never met, okay?

Malcolm X: That's fine. That's the best way.

Crane: All right. Let's start from the beginning. First of all, what is the Black Muslim movement?

Malcolm X: Well, as you know, I'm not in the Black Muslim movement. But the Black Muslim movement is an organization in this country that's headed by Elijah Muhammad.

Crane: That's all?

Malcolm X: It's an organization that's headed by Elijah Muhammad. It says it's a religious organization and that its religion is Islam. But the people in the world of Islam don't accept it as an orthodox Islamic religious organization.

Crane: In other words, they claim to be a branch, an American branch, of the Muhammadan religion.

Malcolm X: No, not the Muhammadan. The real Muslim never refers to his religion as the Muhammadan religion. His religion is Islam.

Crane: Muhammad being the prophet of that—

Malcolm X: Muhammad is one of the prophets of that religion. The people who believe in that religion believe in all of the prophets—Moses, Abraham, Jesus, all of them. But they believe in Muhammad ibn Abd Allah as the last of the prophets. And Elijah Muhammad in this country says that he is also teaching that religion. But that religion is a religion of brotherhood. It advocates the brotherhood of man, all men—

Crane: That's the Muslim religion?

Malcolm X: Yes. This is the—well, those who practice the religion of Islam call themselves Muslims. In this country they're referred to as Moslems.

Crane: Now, you consider yourself to be a Moslem in this country—

Malcolm X: I'm a Moslem. I believe in the religion of Islam.

Crane: And you are no longer a member of the Black Muslims?

Malcolm X: No, no.

Crane: Now what caused that split?

Malcolm X: Well actually, I don't think that it's any— that it contributes anything constructive to go into what caused the split. I'm not in it. I was inseparable from it while I was in it. But now I'm not. I leave it in the past.

Crane: Well, I don't know how valuable it would be— you know, it was inconceivable to think of the Black Muslim movement in this country without thinking of Malcolm X. You were Elijah Muhammad's right-hand man and his leading spokesman, as well as the head of the mosque in New York, which is the largest Black Muslim mosque in the country, as I understood it. And there were certain things that the Black Muslims represented, at least in my mind through your speeches, that I think are worthy of discussion.

Malcolm X: Well, yes. I represented him probably more diligently than all of the rest of his representatives combined. And this somewhat led to the eventual split.

Human nature being what it is—

Crane: Sort of like a power play almost?

Malcolm X: Human nature being what it is.

Crane: Call it politics. We'll call it that.

Malcolm X: Yes.

Crane: But also you said that your trip to Africa has changed your thinking and your position to a great extent.

Malcolm X: Yes. One thing—travel always broadens one's scope. Travel does. . . . Twice this year I visited both Africa and the Middle East. The first time I went was in April and May. I went to Mecca. I went primarily to get a better understanding of Islam.

There were things that happened between me and Elijah Muhammad that caused me to greatly question his ability as a man, much less as a religious leader. And, based upon that doubt, I went in search of an understanding of the religion of Islam. I made the *hajj* or the pilgrimage to Mecca. While I was—one of the things that Elijah Muhammad always taught us was that Islam is a religion of God. It was a religion in which no whites could participate. And he used—to prove his point, he told us that Mecca was a forbidden city. A city that was forbidden to non-Muslims. And since a white person couldn't be a Muslim in his teaching, he said that no white could enter Mecca.

Well, I went to Mecca in May—rather, in April—and everyone was there. In fact one member of the Turkish parliament, who had brought busloads, several hundred busloads, from Turkey to make the pilgrimage, was standing with me on the steps of the hotel in Mina, which is a short distance from Mecca. And he pointed out at that time that Mecca, during the *hajj* season, or the pilgrimage season, would be an anthropologist's paradise, because every specimen of humanity is represented there. It's an absolute brotherhood. So that when I saw this with my own eyes, and saw that people of all colors could practice brotherhood, it was at that point that I wrote back and pointed out that I believed in Islam as a religion of brotherhood.

But this belief in brotherhood doesn't alter the fact that I'm also an Afro-American, or American Negro as you wish, in a society which has very serious and severe race problems which no religion can blind me to.

Crane: Well, what's interesting to me, there are words that you never used to use in the past in our discussions. You never used to use the word *Negro.* That word offended you. You used to say "the so-called Negro"—

Malcolm X: Well, I said Afro-American or American Negro, as you will—

Crane: And you believed also that brotherhood was impossible at one point—

Malcolm X: Let me explain. The reason I say—*Afro-American* is a term that our people in this country increasingly are beginning to use to identify themselves. But in using it, I take into consideration that many people don't know what is meant by Afro-American, so I use the word *Negro* to let you know I was still talking about us. . . .

Crane: Integration offends you. You don't believe in the use of that word. You prefer to think of it as brotherhood which is, for the purposes of our discussion, going to be the same thing. But in the old days you didn't believe in brotherhood, you believed in pure strict separation, didn't you?

Malcolm X: Whenever I opened my mouth, I always said that Elijah Muha—the Honorable Elijah Muhammad—teaches us thus and so. And I spoke for him. I represented him. I represented an organization and organizational thinking. Many of my own views that I had from personal experience I kept to myself. I was faithful to that organization and to that man. Since things came about that made me doubt his integrity, I thought—I think for myself, I listen as much as I can to everyone and try and come up with a capsule opinion, capsulized opinion.

I believe that it is possible for brotherhood to be brought about among all people, but I don't delude myself into dreaming or falling for a dream that this exists before it exists. Some of the American—some of the leaders of our people in this country always say that they, you know, they believe in this dream. But while they're dreaming, our people are having a nightmare, and I don't think that you can make a dream come true by pretending that that dream exists when it doesn't.

Crane: You've been a critic of some of the Negro leadership in this country—Martin Luther King, Roy Wilkins, Abernathy, and others—have you changed in your feelings toward them of late?

Malcolm X: I think all of us should be critics of each other. Whenever you can't stand criticism you can never grow. I don't think that it serves any purpose for the leaders of our people to waste their time fighting each other needlessly. I think that we accomplish more when we sit down in private and iron out whatever differences that may exist and try and then do something constructive for the benefit of our people. But on the other hand, I don't think that we should be above criticism. I don't think that anyone should be above criticism.

Crane: Violence or the threat of violence has always surrounded you. Speeches that you've made have been interpreted as being threats. You have made statements reported in the press about how the Negroes should go out and arm themselves, form militias of their own. I read a thing once, a statement I believe you made that every Negro should belong to the National Rifle Association—

Malcolm X: No, I said this: That in areas of this country where the government has proven its—either its inability or its unwillingness to protect the lives and property of our people, then it's only fair to expect us to do whatever is necessary to protect ourselves. And in situations like Mississippi, places like Mississippi where the government actually has proven its inability to protect us—and it has been proven that ofttimes the police officers and sheriffs themselves are involved in the murder that takes place against our people—then I feel, and I say that anywhere, that our people should start doing what is necessary to protect ourselves. This doesn't mean that we should buy rifles and go out and initiate attacks indiscriminately against whites. But it does mean that we should get whatever is necessary to protect ourselves in a country or in an area where the governmental ability to protect us has broken down—

Crane: Therefore you do not agree with Dr. King's Gandhian philosophy—

Malcolm X: My belief in brotherhood would never restrain me in any way from protecting myself in a society from a people whose disrespect for brotherhood makes them feel inclined to put my neck on a tree at the end of a rope. [*Applause*]

Crane: Well, it sounds as though you could be preaching a sort of an anarchy—

Malcolm X: No, no. I respect government and respect law. But does the government and the law respect us? If the FBI, which is what people depend upon on a national scale to protect the morale and the property and the lives of the people, can't do so when the property and lives of Negroes and whites who try and help Negroes are concerned, then I think that it's only fair to expect elements to do whatever is necessary to protect themselves.

And this is no departure from normal procedure. Because right here in New York City you have vigilante committees that have been set up by groups who see where their neighborhood community is endangered and the law can't do anything about it. So—and even their lives aren't at stake. So—but the fear, Les, seems to come into existence only when someone says Negroes should form vigilante committees to protect their lives and their property.

I'm not advocating the breaking of any laws. But I say that our people will never be respected as human beings until we react as other normal, intelligent human beings do. And this country came into existence by people who were tired of tyranny and oppression and exploitation and the brutality that was being inflicted upon them by powers higher than they, and I think that it is only fair to expect us, sooner or later, to do likewise.

Crane: One last question. You don't preach separatism anymore and I assume you don't want to set up a Black African state in this country anymore. What is your main effort toward now?

Malcolm X: Well, the—one of the organizations which we've now formed, the Organization of Afro-American Unity, has reached the conclusion, after a careful analysis of the problem, that approaching our problem just on the level of civil rights and keeping it within the jurisdiction of the United States will not bring a solution. It's not a Negro problem or an American problem any longer. It's a world problem, it's a human problem. And so we're striving to lift it from the level of civil rights to the level of human rights. And at that level it's international. We can bring it into the United Nations and discuss it in the same tone and in the same language as the problems of people in other parts of the world also is discussed.

Crane: I'm afraid the clock has caught us. It has been interesting. Thank you so much for coming up.

Malcolm X: You're welcome. [*Applause*]

Our people identify with Africa

BERNICE BASS: And now dear hearts, I think it important that we turn to our guest of honor at this time, Minister Malcolm X, the son of a Baptist minister. Good morning.

Malcolm X: How are you, Miss Bass?

Bass: Just fine, thank you. I suppose that's the question New York could ask you after your travels all over the African continent, Europe. We'd love to know exactly what you discovered and what you observed. Whether or not your viewpoints have changed any on the Afro-American questions.

Malcolm X: Well, I've done a lot of traveling and, I think over all, travel does broaden one's scope. If anything at all, that's probably the most important of what's happened to me during the past five or six months.

I was fortunate to be able to spend, I think it was, two months in the Middle East and another two months in the African countries. And I think I visited Egypt, Arabia, Kuwait, Lebanon, and then Sudan, Ethiopia, Kenya, what was then Zanzibar and Tanganyika and is now Tanzania, also Nigeria, Ghana, Liberia, Guinea, and Algiers, or rather Algeria. Then in Europe: Geneva, Paris, and London.

Bass: We who have not traveled have to rely solely on our communications media for the news that we get. What is disturbing and confusing, really, coming out of the African continent, is there unity among the African leaders there? Is there a cohesive effort or is it a divisive thing that has been reported so faithfully in the press, the American press.

Malcolm X: The Western press tries to make it appear that there is a division among Africans. In any bloc or group that has a common objective, you will find disagreements. But overall there's unity. I think—during World War II, America had her allies, and their common objective was to gain victory over a common enemy, but even within that body of allies, there were differences.

Bass: Just as there are today in NATO.

Malcolm X: Certainly, today. But usually Western powers think that they have a priority on the right to differ among themselves. Because when blocs that are other than Western show signs of being able to differ, or differences pop up, the Western press uses this to try and make it appear that they are savage, backward, not able to govern—things of that sort.

Bass: That's something I wanted to ask you about. I've noticed in the last couple of weeks all of the references to the Congo crisis,* when they talked about the debate in the United Nations, they have talked about going back to savagery, tribal practices, this kind of thing. And yet they have in Italy the fact that they have eighteen ballots cast just this week alone trying to elect a premier. They have also—before de Gaulle rose to power, they had a new premier of France every month. And no one considered that backward, and yet these were examples of civilization, culture, and so forth. How do the African delegates

---

* In mid-1964, a revolt broke out in the Congo (today Zaire) led by followers of murdered Prime Minister Patrice Lumumba. They opposed Moise Tshombe becoming prime minister. The U.S.-backed Tshombe had been instrumental in the overthrow of Lumumba's government in 1960. During November 1964, U.S. planes ferried Belgian troops and mercenaries to rebel-held territory in an effort to crush the uprising. These forces carried out a massacre of thousands of Congolese.

in this country and the African leaders in their own countries feel about this kind of characterization?

Malcolm X: Well the—I think this is one of the mistakes the West is making in its efforts to try and win the Africans on their side. The Africans, probably more so than ever before, are beginning to see the deceit and the double standard of measurement that's used when their own case is involved. And how it differs from that when the African case is involved. And this has gone a long ways toward making Africans question the motive of Western powers, including the United States.

It's not an accident that in the United Nations during this present session, for the first time during the nineteen or twenty years that the UN has been in existence, we find African foreign ministers who are openly accusing the United States of being an imperialist power and of practicing racism. In the past, these labels were always confined to the European colonial powers. But never was the United States itself singled out and labeled, identified as an imperialist power.

Neither was the case of Black people in this country ever linked with what was happening to people on the African continent. And if there's any drastic departure from past procedures that have been reflected already in the present UN session, it's the tendency on the part of African representatives one after another all to link what's happening in the Congo with what's happening in Mississippi.

And for the first time, too, since the UN has been in existence, we have representatives of foreign governments referring to the releasing of the twenty-one assassins of the civil rights workers. This was mentioned in the United Nations Security Council debate this week.

And so all of this is a sign, or reflects the tendency on the part of Africans to identify completely with what is happening to the Black man in this country. And they also realize that there's an increasing tendency on the part of our people in this country to identify with what's going on or happening to our people on the African continent.

And never are our people given the real picture. One thing I will say for James Farmer, with whom I was in a discussion earlier this week. He is going to Africa. One radio report—I was riding home in my car one night, and I heard a radio newscaster say that James Farmer was going to Africa to counteract the false conceptions that I had given during my trip.

Well, I called Farmer the next day. First I was in—I was irked, I was irritated, I was very angry. But then I began to remember what the press had done to me and done to others in trying to divide and conquer, and I called Mr. Farmer. And he said he knew absolutely nothing about what this particular newscaster had reported.

And then I had a personal conversation with him a little later on, which I found to be very intelligent and very objective on his part. And he explained then that he was going to take a fact-finding trip to Africa, and visit many of these places. And he done so under the auspices of the Big Six to find out—they want to know for themselves the African story.* And whether or not the news of Africa is being properly reported in this country. Which I think is a very progressive move on the part of those people who have been set up to lead Black people in this country.

Bass: Was this an outgrowth of—I think they've had two meetings—all of the Big Six in Washington, members of the State Department, and so forth, and African representatives—in the attempt to bridge the gap.

Malcolm X: Because those who are invited are able to see that the problem of the Black people in this country is not an isolated problem. It's not a Negro problem or an American problem. It's part of the world problem. It's a human problem.

---

* The "Big Six" were the chief leaders of the civil rights movement.

Bass: May I ask you this—can I interrupt you a moment to ask you this: I'm concerned over the habit that the communications media has picked up of identifying Black people in Africa as Negroes and then Black people here as Negroes. . . .

Malcolm X: Well, that's because at one time Africa, the word *African,* was used in this country in a derogatory way. But now, since Africa has gotten—it's getting its independence and there are so many independent African states. The image of the African has changed from negative to positive. And the white man in this country does not like to give us anything positive that we can identify with. And since he can't stop the independence movement of the people on that continent, he's trying to change the label. Trying to change that which they call themselves to put them in the same category with us. But I don't think they'll be very successful at that.

Bass: Well, how do the African delegates in this country and the people, the leaders, how do they feel about it?

Malcolm X: They don't accept the word *Negro* at all. No one accepts the word *Negro* but our people in this country, and it's only because we've been mistaught, misguided, misled, and misinformed.

Bass: We've reached a very good point at which to pause in order to identify both the program and the station. By this time you know this is "Community Corner" here in New York City and your hostess for this period as she has been for the last three-and-a-half years is Bernice Bass and our guest here is the son of a Baptist minister, the Honorable Minister Malcolm X. . . .

Malcolm X: I never accept the term *honorable.*

Bass: That's a beautiful title.

Malcolm X: Well, I'll tell you. Most people I've seen really end up misusing it, and I'd rather just be your brother Malcolm.

Bass: I've got a big family, but I can always use additional. I hope my mother will not be disturbed about it—but I find most people are honorable, whether they wear the title or not. We have a few brothers who aren't. Getting back to what you saw when you were in Africa, how are the countries developing and how—when you hear all this business about the tremendous amount of aid that the United States is giving all of these countries. Are they developing? What plans do they have?

Malcolm X: Yes, one of the countries developing the most swiftly is Egypt. Egypt's development is tremendous and also Ghana. Ghana, probably, and Egypt are the forefront. Ghana is a remarkable country, a remarkably progressive country.

And I think that it might even interest you, and by the way, it might interest you to know that one of the most progressive moves Ghana has made is to start establishing, installing, a television network. And I was taken through this television studio and plant by Mrs. Du Bois, Dr. W.E.B. Du Bois's wife, who is the director of television in Ghana. She—to my knowledge, she's the only Black director of television in Africa. I may be wrong, but the only one I know of is she. And she's a woman, and she's an Afro-American, and I think that should make Afro-American women mighty proud.

She's one of the most intelligent women I've ever met, and not only is she the director of television, but she took me on a tour of Tema, which is a new industrial city. It's a new city that has been set up by President [Kwame] Nkrumah which has the most advanced type of machinery and everything else in it. And one of the things that exists in this city is the publishing plant—the most modern publishing plant on the African continent. The machines are tremendous, and it can reproduce any type of magazine, book, or newspaper in the best form and of the best quality. And there are many other aspects of the Ghanaian life that I found to be quite progressive.

I was saying—if I may continue—I was in a hotel in Cairo, the Shepheard's Hotel in Cairo, and there was a group of students that had traveled the African continent from a certain college here in this country. And Africa was their last stop before embarking for the States. I was in conversation with some of them in the lobby of the Shepheard's and they were conveying some of their impressions. And they were greatly enthused over [President Léopold] Senghor in Senegal, collectively. And they were, at the same time, disillusioned with Nkrumah in Ghana, collectively. They had a tendency to criticize and condemn Nkrumah, but at the same time pat Senghor of Senegal on the back. Later on in the conversation, while they were pointing out the negative conditions that existed in Senegal—how Dakar had poverty, beggars, and things of that sort—and at the same time they were speaking of the actions of beggars and the progressiveness of the Ghanaian people and how they all looked industrious and seemed to be making a contribution to the whole overall forward movement—progressive movement forward.

So I answered that. These were students. How could they say that Senghor was such a great president and at the same time speak of the negative conditions that his people were in and also turn around and say that they have criticisms for Nkrumah? They have to admit that the negative conditions didn't exist in Nkrumah's country. So, what I gather from this, that their yardstick of measurement for leadership was not what the leader was doing for his people and his country, but the attitude that that particular leader had toward this country and the attitude that this country had toward that leader.

They weren't using a real yardstick to measure that person's abilities. So I thought I would throw this in because to me it was quite indicative of the entire attitude of the power structure here toward the African countries and African leaders. If African leaders are manipulated—if they can be manipulated by the power structure here, no matter how negative the conditions remain in that particular leader's country, this power structure turns its propaganda machine for the benefit, for the benefit of that African leader. But by the same token, if it's an African leader that they can't manipulate and use as a puppet, then they turn their propaganda machine upon that particular leader and make him appear as a dictator or some type of monstrosity and misinform and mislead the American public this way.

Bass: May I ask you—one of the points that you have not yet made in regard to that problem is the fact that the Ghanaian women there seem to be emerging on the scene at all levels.

Malcolm X: One thing I noticed in both the Middle East and Africa, in every country that was progressive, the women were progressive. In every country that was underdeveloped and backward, it was to the same degree that the women were undeveloped, or underdeveloped, and backward.

Bass: What you're saying is the women are actually playing a part there, in Africa?

Malcolm X: Well, no, I'm saying this: That it's noticeable that in these type of societies where they put the woman in a closet and discourage her from getting a sufficient education and don't give her the incentive by allowing her maximum participation in whatever area of the society where she's qualified, they kill her incentive. And killing her incentive, she kills the incentive in her children. And the man himself has no competition so he doesn't develop to his fullest potential. So in the African countries where they opt for mass education, whether it be female or male, you find that they have a more valid society, a more progressive society. And Ghana is one of the best examples of this. Egypt was also another example of this.

Bass: Well, certainly. I remember when the White Paper came out issued by Kwame Nkrumah on this business of polygamy. There was a great deal of talk, discussion back and forth, and I remember I interviewed a young lady from the Ghanaian embassy here and—is polygamy—was it there or did you get a chance to notice it?

Malcolm X: Well, how would you know? I didn't have any yardstick that I could use to determine—

Bass: I thought in conversation, not actual—

Malcolm X: Well, their conversation differs from the conversation over here. They aren't so inclined to talk about their—

Bass: Personal lives—

Malcolm X:—as is the case in this society.

Bass: Well, isn't that funny. Now, I'm thinking of [name unintelligible], I think, from here at the United Nations from Nigeria. He stirred a great deal of controversy when he came out in favor of [polygamy] when he was speaking before a women's group pressing for women's rights at the United Nations.

Malcolm X: Well, he stirred up even more controversy this time by pressing for United States' right to drop bombs on defenseless African villages.

Bass: Well, I'm telling you—you've been talking about Ghana. How does Ghana compare to Nigeria in terms of development, in terms of their handling of national affairs and that sort of thing?

Malcolm X: Well, the Nigerian people are great. You never can find any people anywhere in Africa more hospitable and brotherly and who will welcome you more warmly than the people in Nigeria. But by the same token the United States influence in Nigeria has turned it almost into a colony. And there are conditions that exist in Nigeria that are very explosive. They're getting ready to have elections this week, which could turn Nigeria into another Congo.

Nigeria is one of the richest countries on the African continent—one of the most beautiful of the African countries. But by the same token you'll find beggars there, you find poverty there. You don't find new cities. You find beggars and poverty in Lagos, which you don't see in Ghana.

I don't in any way condemn or criticize the Nigerian people. I think Nigeria's problems stem primarily from the overexertion on the part of outside interests. The United States presence in Nigeria is far beyond what it should be, and its influence is far beyond what it should be.

I might say, Miss Bass, in most of the African countries that are the most pro-American or the most inseparably interwoven into the American way of thought, you find that the conditions, economic conditions, of those countries are usually the worst.

Bass: Like Liberia.

Malcolm X: Well, name whichever you like. But you'd be surprised. The countries that are identified with America the most are the ones that are the most backward and the ones that have the most problems.

Bass: Now the ones that are the most progressive, they are most closely identified with what power?

Malcolm X: Well, they're more closely identified with themselves. I don't think that one can—there's a tendency here in America again, to try and project any African nation that isn't on America's apron strings as linked with some other power. But the Africans themselves want to be Africans. They don't want to be identified with any of the what's known as European philosophies or Occidental or Western philosophies. They want what's good for Africa. They want to take out of any other philosophy that which they can adopt to their own needs and to their own development. But to be identified with either the Communist bloc or the capitalist bloc, I don't think you'll find any African country or African leader who will buy that—he's for Africa.

And during the five weeks that I was there, I took some excellent movies, by the way, which I'm going to show at the Audubon Ballroom this time Friday night. I took movies in Egypt that were—I think no one else has them. I'll just say that they're unique—exclusives, yes. I was at the 23d of July independence celebration in Egypt when Haile Selassie, President Nkrumah, all of the heads of state were there. And they were watching President Nasser's display of weaponry that is unequaled on the African continent. You've got to see these films to see the massive military might that President Gamal Abdel Nasser has developed there in Egypt. Then you can see why he's in a position to openly state that he will support the Congo freedom fighters, and you can also see why it caused so much concern here in the West.

Bass: But now I'd ask you—at the same time he announced his intention to do that, he's also stepping up his request for aid from the United States to the tune of 35 to 40 billion dollars in surplus food.

Malcolm X: President Nasser took all of the aid that was forthcoming from Russia to build the Aswan Dam and turned around and put the Communists in jail in his country. Which shows he doesn't take aid to—for those countries to tell him what he can do. If they're interested in objectively contributing to the development of his country and his people, then he takes the aid. He'll take American aid with no strings attached. But if there are strings attached, he does exactly what he says in the paper, he tells them to go jump in the lake.

Bass: Well, that's interesting. Except that—you begin to wonder when it's done on an international level, not just with Nasser but all the others, too. Practical reality tells you, you can't get something for nothing. And when they come after you for money or aid or what have you, what are they giving in return? I can't understand—

Malcolm X: You've got to consider that these Western powers are in the economic position of strength that exists in their countries today only because of their past exploitation of these same areas. They're not giving aid, they're only returning some of what was taken.

Bass: But in business, you don't do this. You know what I mean. What you're saying anyhow talking about a moral right and I agree—

Malcolm X: I don't talk moral—

Bass: But I'm talking about a practical business standpoint. I have amassed so many billions of dollars. You are now struggling. You are asking for a loan. I can or cannot give—

Malcolm X: One of the reasons I'm struggling is because you took from me the—

Bass: Ah ha.

Malcolm X:—the billions of dollars that you have.

Bass: You know, somebody once said—not talking about the international scene—but they once said that if all the wealth in the world were divided equally, in a matter of years or in a specified amount of time, most of the people who had the wealth previously would have it again.

Malcolm X: That's because most of them who have it are more shrewd at thievery and those other things that bring it about.

Bass: Now, when all these other countries begin to get as prosperous as the Western powers, will they then be accused of having gotten that way through thievery or will theirs be shrewdness and cunning?

Malcolm X: Well, you see these people—look at in terms of business. In business it's called profit sharing. And—

Bass: I wonder—

Malcolm X: If you check today's *New York Times,* they're saying the Egyptian situation with Gamal Abdel Nasser—in the Sunday *Times* it was—Arnold Toynbee, he is supposed to be one of the brains in this era, he says, and I quote: "Dr. Toynbee regards the Middle East as an area of growing importance. 'Nasser has been tactless in his dealings with other Arab leaders, but he is the first ruler to do anything for the Egyptian peasants. The pyramids were built for the rulers of Egypt, but the

Aswan High Dam for the good of the people. Nasser will continue to be a big force in the Arab world; I myself rather like and admire him. I've noticed quite a prejudice against Nasser in this country, Americans seem to assume that he is a dictator, a bad man. I don't agree with that.'" This is Toynbee.

Bass: Yes, I know. He used to say about two or three years ago, in talking about Martin Luther King—said that in his opinion, his espousal of nonviolence was perhaps one of the savings of Christianity in the Western world.

Malcolm X: It probably would be the savings of Christianity in the Western world, even if it wasn't the savings of the Negroes—

Bass: No, he didn't say Negroes. He said Christianity. . . . I'd like to know about the impact of the various American missionaries, all the religious feeling, on the African continent. I find that in other reports that have come in, that Islam, the religion of Islam, seems to be making great strides and Christianity is not doing very well there, and I wonder, why?

Malcolm X: This is true. The religion of Islam has spread rapidly in Africa and is still spreading quite rapidly in Africa. It's a very powerful force. And the religion of Christianity has run into what you might call a stone wall. There's a tendency on the part of our people in that area to link Christianity with the European colonial powers that have dominated and exploited these past years. And Islam is a religion that's won more acceptance. It's easier to fit, it fits right in to the nature of one's everyday life. In fact it's a natural religion. It's a religion that's easier to practice.

Bass: Well, let me see—and I'm trying to remember now—who was it who said one of the missionaries was talking about his impressions of Africa—I've forgotten what country it was involved at the time—that when he got there he was surprised to find other missionaries who were teaching the natives Christianity, insisting on the natives coming through the back door while their white compatriots came through the front door. And this new white missionary to Africa found this a bit strange, since they were all reading the same Bible.

Malcolm X: Well, this is why Islam is spreading. Islam has no color bar in it at all. Islam has no—there's nothing in Islam that teaches one to judge a man by the color of his skin. No matter what color you are in Islam—you're a Muslim, you're a brother.

Bass: That's interesting, hearing you say that, in view of some of your former statements—

Malcolm X: Well, notice all of my former statements were prefaced by "the Honorable Elijah Muhammad teaches thus and so." They weren't my statements, they were his statements, and I was repeating them.

Bass: Parroting them. The same thing you accuse Judge Thurgood Marshall of doing once upon a time.

Malcolm X: And now the parrot has jumped out of the cage.

Bass: Well, that's interesting, we're going to see what else he does. [*Laughter*] Good morning. . . .

Caller: I'm calling from Manhattan. I would like to ask: Why do the Arabs discriminate against the Black man? And especially I read about the Sudan where they attacked and killed Negroes just because they were black.

Bass: Perhaps Minister Malcolm X can answer that.

Malcolm X: My own—when I was in East Africa, I noticed that there was a strong feeling among the Africans along the East African coast against the Asians. When I went to West Africa, I noticed that there was a strong feeling among the Africans against the Arabs. And in parts of Africa where there were neither Asians or Arabs, I noticed a strong feeling among Africans—if they were Muslim, it was against Africans who were Christian, or if they were Christian, it was against Africans who were Muslim.

And when you study the divisive forces at work on the African continent today, you'll find that these divisive forces are not indigenous to the African or the African continent, but they are coming from outside. And the powers that have ruled Africa in the past are aware that the real independence of Africa began to take its impetus from the Bandung Conference,[*] which was a forging together of the Asian-Arab-African bloc. And this bloc, with no nuclear weapons or weapons of modern warfare, were able to gain a great deal toward independence against the European powers, because of their numerical strength, their unity.

So these powers realize that they've been pushed against the wall during recent years and the only weapon that they have against this force that has been pushing them against the wall is divide and conquer—the tactic that they've always used. So that, if I may finish, so that in every area where you find people who have been colonized and oppressed today striving toward freedom, you find that whereas in the past they got along, today they're fighting each other. Just like in British Guiana—it's the Asians against the Black man. And this is not indigenous trouble that stems from the people themselves. It's instigated by outside forces. And then it's blown up to give the impression that the fight that's going on among them or between them is something other than what it actually is.

Bass: May I ask you this—now you say this is not indigenous to the African continent and then of course, you just mentioned British Guiana. But if you look at history, don't you find that all continents or all groups of people in a wide geographical area usually come up with differences within themselves—Canada for instance, the United States. It's not just Africa alone.

---

[*] See note on page 51.

Malcolm X: Certainly. But when these differences come up and they are normal, or natural—

Bass: Hold on just a minute.

Malcolm X: —you'll find that they usually take a different pattern than that which is developing on the African continent or in British Guiana. Because if the Asians and the Blacks in British Guiana could live so much in harmony together when the British were there, you tell me why now that the British are being pushed out, or they're being threatened with being pushed out, that all of a sudden the power that could push them out—instead of pushing them out begins to fight among themselves. This is not an accident. And the same pattern is developing in different parts of the world. It's divide and conquer.

Bass: Does that answer your question, sir?

Caller: Ma'am, for clearness' sake you should also talk about the Arabs. I think for clearness' sake you should also mention the Arab role in—as slave traders and the hatred that would stem from that.

Bass: Did you hear that, Minister Malcolm X? Now we're going to hang up, but he's going to answer that.

Malcolm X: I don't condone slavery, no matter who it's carried on by. And I think that—I don't condone slavery no matter who carries it on. And I think that every power that has participated in slavery of any form on this earth, in history, has paid for it, except the United States. All of your European powers that colonized, your—the part that the Arabs played in the enslavement of Africans, all of them who played a part have lost their empire, lost their power, lost their position, except the United States. The United States was the recipient of the slaves, and she's the only one up till now who has yet to pay.

Bass: Do you want—what's your prognosis for the future as regards the United States, as we get ready to leave our breathless listening audience?

Malcolm X: The Bible, in the Book of Revelations, says he that leads into captivity shall go into captivity. This is in the thirteenth chapter, the one that the preacher thought didn't exist. It says he who leads into captivity shall go into captivity. He who kills by the sword shall be killed by the sword. This is justice. So I don't think that any power can enslave a people and not look forward to having that justice come back upon itself.

Bass: Well, Minister Malcolm X, thank you for visiting. We need to have you back time and time and time again so that we can eventually touch on some of the points of interest that intrigue our listening audience. Now we don't want our listeners to forget that you are going to be showing movies taken on your trip at the Audubon Ballroom at—what time?—

Malcolm X: At eight o'clock Sunday night, the Audubon Ballroom.

Bass: At eight o'clock Sunday night, here in New York City. Minister Malcolm X himself. . . .

PART 3

February 1965: Two speeches delivered during the last week of Malcolm X's life

Until Malcolm X lost his position as minister of Elijah Muhammad's New York City mosque, the Nation of Islam had provided him with a rent-free home. But after Malcolm left the Nation, it instituted legal proceedings to recover possession of the dwelling. Malcolm lost the lawsuit. His able attorney, Percy Sutton, did his best to postpone the date of eviction.

Then, at 2:30 a.m. on February 14, 1965, a Molotov cocktail–caused fire destroyed part of his home. The Nation of Islam insisted that Malcolm had set the fire himself, partly to obtain publicity, partly to deprive his Muslim rivals of the use of the house. Malcolm ridiculed the claim. "Let the chips fall where they may," he exclaimed on February 15 at an Organization of Afro-American Unity meeting of more than 500 people at Harlem's Audubon Ballroom. He said the Nation was more interested in fighting other Blacks than it was in combating the Ku Klux Klan.

Despite warnings that the Nation would not tolerate such statements, Malcolm X continued to press the attack. He held Elijah Muhammad's movement responsible for the bombing and characterized it as "a criminal organization."

On February 16, 1965, Malcolm addressed a predominantly Black audience in Rochester. Five days later, he was assassinated in New York City.

February 1965.
(Photo: New York
Daily News)

There's a worldwide revolution going on

A
S MANY of you probably know, tonight we were going to unfold a program which we felt would be beneficial to the struggle of our people in this country. But because of events which are beyond our control we have—we feel that it is best to postpone unfolding the program that we had in mind until a later date.*

Sunday morning about three o'clock, somebody threw some bombs inside my house. Normally I wouldn't get excited over a few bombs, but the ones who threw these not only aimed them in rooms where there—where there was no one, but even in rooms where three of my daughters sleep. One daughter six, one daughter four, and one daughter two. And since I am, am quite certain that those who threw the bombs knew my house well enough to know where everyone was sleeping, I can't quite bring my heart to the point where it can in any way be merciful, or from now on compromising, toward anyone who can be that low. Especially when I heard on the news today that Joseph, a brother that I found in the garbage can in Detroit in 1952—that's where I found him [*Laughter*]—made the statement that I had bombed my own house.

---

* The "Basic Unity Program" of the Organization of Afro-American Unity can be found in George Breitman, *The Last Year of Malcolm X: The Evolution of a Revolutionary* (New York: Pathfinder, 1967), pp. 113-24.

Now you see, this doesn't surprise me, because I know that since many of us left the Muslim movement, its intelligence and its morals have gone bankrupt. Both its intelligence and its morals have gone bankrupt.

And now they are using the same tactics that's used by the Ku Klux Klan. When the Klan bombs your church, they say you did it. When they bomb the synagogue, they say the Jews bombed their own synagogue. This is a Klan tactic. And to me—I'll tell you why the Black Muslim movement is now adopting the same tactic against Black people as has been up to now the exclusive method of the Ku Klux Klan.

I want to point out, too, that I'm not talking about Muslims just to make white people happy. Because I don't believe in letting anyone use me against somebody else. I'm telling you these things because I have reached a point where I feel that Black people in this country need to know what's going on. And I'm talking about an organization which I had a hand in building, which I had a hand in organizing. I know its characteristics. I know its potential. I know its behavior patterns. I know what it can do and what it cannot do. One of the things it can do is bomb your house and try to kill your baby.

Before we get into it, I would like to point out also, as many of you know, last Tuesday, or last weekend, I was invited to address the first congress of the Council of African Organizations in London. They had a four-day congress on the fifth, sixth, seventh, and eighth and had invited me there to make the closing address and bring the delegates from the various African organizations that are situated on the European continent up to date in regards to the struggle of the Black man in this country in his quest for human rights and human dignity. And in conjunction with that invitation, I had gotten an invitation to visit Paris from the Afro-American community in Paris, which was sponsoring a rally in conjunction with the African community. And I was supposed to go there

Tuesday also and address them and let them know the state of development or lack of development of our progress in this country for human rights, or toward human rights.

As many of you know, when I got to Paris, the man said I couldn't come in—some man. French man! They gave me no explanation other than that they—we have our own. They wouldn't let me phone the American embassy. And they tried to imply that the American embassy was behind it, which—I told them that I didn't know de Gaulle had become a satellite of Lyndon B. Johnson. I knew that Kennedy had made a satellite out of Khrushchev and half of—and Britain—and half of these other countries, and I didn't think that France was a satellite of the United States.

Well, it made them angry because they like to be independent, you know—or pretend to be independent. But they wouldn't let me in. They wouldn't let me phone the American embassy.

And later on, when I got back in London—and by the way, when I got back to London there was about twenty different delegates who were delegates from about twenty different African organizations on hand at the airport, and they were going to raise hell if anything had happened other than what should have happened. As it was, I ended back—I reentered England with no trouble and immediately got in telephone contact with the brothers and sisters who were in Paris. And they pointed out that they had encountered some difficulty, first from the Communist trade union workers. Now mind you, Communist trade union workers had prevented them from renting their hall, and when they went to get another hall the same Communist group had exercised its influence to prevent them from getting that hall.

Finally, when they did get a hall, evidently someone was strong enough to exercise influence over the French government. And I might add that while I was in custody of the French, every time I made a request, before they would say yes or no, they telephoned the French foreign ministry. So that they were taking their orders from someone high up in the French foreign ministry who did not want me to enter France.

And there's a reason for it. I don't blame them [*Laughter*] because—and I told the parties there—I said maybe my plane got mixed up and I was in South Africa, in the wrong country. . . . This couldn't be Paris, it must be Johannesburg. And they got red. And you know how they can get red. [*Laughter*] One of them was pink. [*Laughter*]

The same thing happened in England, as many of you probably read in the Sunday *Times* and the *Tribune*. There was a great fear in England concerning me speaking to the West Indian community. And because—this is because England has a very serious color problem developing, because so many of our people are migrating there from the British West Indies. France, quietly as it is kept, has a very serious color problem developing because of the migration to France of our people from the French West Indies.

And with these people from the French West Indies, Black people going to France, others from the British West Indies going to England, coupled with the Asians who are coming from the Commonwealth territory, along with the Africans from French Equatorial West Africa [coming] into France, and the British possessions into Britain, there's a large, increasing number of dark-skinned people swelling the dark population of France and Britain. And it's giving them a great deal of horror of the world—the only difference over there and over here being that no one of black skin in France has ever tried to unite the dark-skinned people together. Neither have they done so in England. So you can somewhat see what their fear is.

No effort has been made to unite the Afro-American community or the American Negro community with the

West Indian community and then those two communities with the African community, and both communities with the Asian community. This has never been done, in neither England or France. But when I was in France in November just for a few days, I was successful in getting a few of the Afro-Americans who live there together, and they formed a branch of the OAAU, the Organization of Afro-American Unity. And as soon as they formed this branch, they began to work in conjunction with the African organization and became a power that had to be reckoned with. And this is what the French government did not want.

Also the same thing in Britain. The West Indian community is very restless, or rather, yes, restless and dissatisfied. And they too are trying to organize or find someone who can bring them together. And this has caused in England a great deal of fear, a great deal of concern. And the effect of it is that it makes them act in a very silly way sometimes.

Now, to leave that for a moment. As you'll recall, when I was in Mecca in September, I wrote back a letter which was printed in the *New York Times* in which I pointed out that it was my intention when I returned to expose Elijah Muhammad as a religious faker.* This is what I wrote. [*Applause*] Now, while I was in Mecca among the Muslims, I had a chance to meditate and think and see things with a great deal of clarity—with much greater clarity than I've achieved from over here, entangled with all this mess that we are confronted by constantly. And I had made up my mind, yes, that I was going to tell the

---

* An article titled "Malcolm Rejects Racist Doctrine" in the October 4, 1964, *New York Times* quoted Malcolm as writing "to a friend in New York" that "this religion recognizes all men as brothers. It accepts all human beings as equals before God, and as equal members in the Human Family of Mankind. I totally reject Elijah Muhammad's racist philosophy, which he has labeled 'Islam'. . . ."

Black people in the Western Hemisphere, who I had played a great role in misleading into the hands of Elijah Muhammad, exactly what kind of man he was and what he was doing.

And I might point out right here that it was not a case of my knowing all the time, because I didn't. I had blind faith in him, the same as many of you have had and still have blind faith in me or blind faith in Moses or blind faith in somebody else. My faith in Elijah Muhammad was more blind and more uncompromising than any faith that any man has ever had for another man. And so I didn't try to see him as he actually was. But, being away, I could see him better, understand many things better.

And, well, when I came back to this country, as you recall, I was very quiet. I knew the best thing was when they tried to ask me questions about him, I ducked it. I didn't want to get involved. I didn't want to get into it. Well, the reason for that was this: The letter that I wrote was written when I was in Arabia, in September, whereas, after leaving Arabia I had gone into Africa. I had had an opportunity to hold long discussions with President Julius Nyerere in what is now Tanzania; with Jomo Kenyatta, the president of Kenya, the Republic of Kenya; long discussions with Prime Minister Milton Obote of Uganda; President Azikiwe of Nigeria; President Nkrumah of Ghana; and President Sékou Touré in Guinea. And the understanding that I had in conversations with these men is that they are great men. The understanding that I got broadened my scope so much that I felt I could see the problems and complaints of Black people in America and the Western Hemisphere with much greater clarity.

And I felt foolish coming back to this country and getting into a little two-bit argument with some bird-brained person who calls himself a Black Muslim. I felt I was wasting my time. I felt it would be a drag for me to come back here and allow myself to be in a whole lot of public arguments and physical fisticuffs—knowing what I knew, and knowing that it would actually be more beneficial to our people if a constructive program were put in front of them immediately.

Many of you will recall that shortly after I came back, despite the fact that I said nothing about the Black Muslims, a wire was put in the newspaper under the name of Raymond Sharrieff threatening me if I were to say anything about Elijah Muhammad. Actually that wasn't Raymond Sharrieff's wire, that was Elijah Muhammad's wire. Raymond Sharrieff has no words of his own.

If you recall, when I was in the Black Muslim movement, I never said anything without saying Elijah Muhammad seems to believe thus and so, or Elijah Muhammad said thus and so. This is the way the Black Muslim movement is organized. Nobody makes any public statement unless it comes from Elijah Muhammad. And nobody makes any move unless it comes from Elijah Muhammad. They didn't do it then and they don't do it now.

So, when Raymond Sharrieff put that letter in the paper—that wire, rather, in the paper—that wire was from Elijah Muhammad himself. And he was trying to irk me into saying something so that a public hullabaloo would take place again because they wanted to jockey me into the same position I was in before I left the country.

Before I left the country, I had permitted them to jockey me into a position—me and the good brothers and sisters who also had sense enough to leave from down there—I was foolish enough to let them jockey me into a position where we were taking potshots at each other, so to speak, and it was known throughout the country that the Muslims in the temple were trying to do this thing.

So it put me in a spot where anybody could do it and then blame it on those foolish Muslims. And I was well aware of this. So, by staying away for four or five months, that ended. But when I came back, being quiet, they wanted the same thing again. They wanted some more hullabaloo so that it would appear that the Black Muslims were going to do this and the Black Muslims were going to do that and then anybody could do it and blame those fools and they wouldn't have sense enough to see it. You can understand that can't you? And when I say anybody, I mean anybody. But I know who those anybodies are. [*Laughter*]

I continue to concentrate, continue to ignore them and concentrate on trying to get the Organization of Afro-American Unity better organized. Because I knew that and I felt that what it had in mind would actually solve the problems of many of our people—most of our people.

If you'll notice—and, but despite the fact that I tried to keep quiet, on January 22 I came out of my house one night and they jumped me, on a Friday night, about 11:15. Now, I knew that they weren't out there waiting for me, because normally I wouldn't come out at that time of the night. So that when I did come out and ran into them and they did jump me, I knew then that they were casing my house. And frankly, I waited for them for a month. I'd sit around that house with my rifle; stayed up all times of the night just to get one chance to put somebody in hell. [*Laughter*] Just one chance. [*Applause*]

I warned my wife at that time that they were casing the house. Again, I know their behavior. And I also became more careful, wherever I would go and whenever I would go anywhere. And then to make it worse, when I went to Los Angeles a couple of weeks ago, they had gotten so insane that they chased me right down the Hollywood Freeway in broad daylight. Yes! Now, the thing that you have to consider about this is, the police were at the airport. The police knew what they were up to. In fact, the police arrested a couple of them in front of someone's home the night before. They knew all about it. Nothing was said in the paper. Now, imagine someone is chasing you down the Hollywood Freeway at eighty miles an hour and it doesn't get in the paper. No.

So later on—that was on a Thursday. Friday I was in Chicago. I appeared on the Kup [Irv Kupcinet] show. And when I went on the Kup show I had about twenty police. There were twenty police out there guarding the station. It might seem odd, but the Muslims were there. And they even tried to attack the police, which was never put in the paper. They followed the police, because of that—they act kind of nuts. And I'm so thankful that I'm out of there, I don't expect. . . . [*Laughter*] Because I was the same kind of nut. I was just as nuts as they were. If Elijah Muhammad had told me to go get somebody's head, I would have gone and gotten it just like that. And that's what's the matter with them. They're only following what I taught them how to do. So, I understand. [*Laughter*]

But despite the fact that they put on this performance, it was quieted down. Nothing was said about it. And then the night I was on the Susskind show, the David Susskind Show, those same persons were—had surrounded the station. They had even almost strong-armed the police. The police didn't do a thing to strike back at them. They almost strong-armed them. Nothing was done about that. But while I was on the . . . show they had come to the studio and told Susskind that I wasn't going to be down there that night. And told him that I would never make it. But, again, I know how they do, and I, thanks to Allah, did something other than what they expected.

So, the next thing that irritated them and irritated them the most was this. And I've been doing it for a month, and nobody knew why I was doing it. You notice, I had shifted my attack from them to Rockwell and the Ku Klux Klan.* For the past month I've been beating on

---

* George Lincoln Rockwell headed the American Nazi Party, which later became the National Socialist White People's Party.

the Klan and beating on Rockwell and beating on these so-called right-wingers. You may wonder why. I sent a wire to Rockwell warning him if anything happened to Black people in Alabama that we would give him maximum retaliation. The press knew it. You heard nothing about it. Rockwell disappeared because he's scared of power like anybody else. Because they know that he has strength only as long as he's dealing with somebody that's nonviolent. Good Lord. [*Applause*]

Rockwell and his whole crowd agree only as long as they're dealing with someone nonviolent. The Ku Klux Klan and that crowd agree only when they're dealing with someone nonviolent. Citizens' Council and that crowd agree only when they're dealing with someone that's nonviolent. And you know it.

So, he cleared out. I went to Alabama. I went to Alabama purposely to see what was happening down there. While I was there, I wasn't trying to interfere with King's program, whatever it was. He was in jail. I talked, I spoke at Tuskegee, [*Laughter*] I spoke at Tuskegee Institute last Tuesday night, I think it was. There were over 3,000 students and others. And it was the students themselves that night who insisted that I go with them the next morning to Selma, some students from SNCC. So I went. After giving it careful thought, I went.

When I got to Selma, the press began to bug me right away. And I wouldn't even tell them my name. I just ignored them completely. So they insisted that I hold a press conference. I didn't ask for a press conference. They insisted that I hold a press conference. Which was held. And while the press was there, the Klan was there. When you're looking at the cops in Alabama, you're looking at the Klan. That's who the Klan is. [*Applause*]

Knowing where I was, right then and there, I reminded Lyndon B. Johnson of the promise he had made to good, well-meaning Americans when he was running for president. He said that if he were elected he would pull the sheets off the Ku Klux Klan. Did he not say that? Yes, he did. So, here you've got Klansmen knocking little babies down the road with a. . . . You've got Klansmen knocking Black women down in front of a camera and that poor fool Black man standing on the sidelines because he's nonviolent. Now, we don't go along with a thing like that. [*Applause*]

Well, it was then, in Selma, Alabama, in front of the face of the Ku Klux Klan that I demanded in your name, the Organization of Afro-American Unity—could I make that demand in your name? [*Applause*]—that since 97 percent of the Black people in this country had supported Lyndon B. Johnson and his promise, and now that his party has the largest majority that any president has had in a long time, Lyndon B. Johnson is obligated to the Black man in this country to put up an immediate federal commission to investigate the Ku Klux Klan, which is a criminal organization organized to murder and maim and cripple Black people in this country.

And, I pointed out that if Lyndon B. Johnson could not keep his promise and expose the Ku Klux Klan, then we would be within our rights to come to Alabama and organize the Black people of Alabama and pull the sheets off the Klan ourselves. [*Applause*] And we can do it. Brothers and sisters, we can do it. And the federal government won't do it. Since then, they've been talking about a little investigation of the Klan and the Citizens' Council and the Black Muslims and some of the others. But they're not going to do anything. The only way the Klan is going to be stopped is when you and I organize and stop them ourselves. Yes, that's what's out there. [*Applause*]

You may say, well, why am I so down on the Klan all of a sudden? I'm going to tell you why. And why did I shift my attack from the Black Muslims—Elijah Muhammad and his immoral self—to the Klan? Yes, he's immoral. You can't take nine teenaged women and seduce them and give them babies and not tell me you're—and then tell me you're moral. You could do it if you admitted you did it and admitted that the babies were yours. I'd shake your hand and call you a man. A good one too. [*Laughter*] Any time you seduce teenaged girls and make them be childs with adultery, make them hide your crimes, why, you're not even a man, much less a divine man. [*Laughter*]

So, and this is what he did. He took at least nine that we know about. And I'm not speculating, because he told this to me himself. Yes, that's why he wants me dead because he knew as soon as I walked out that I'd tell it. Nine of them. Not two of them who are suing him, but nine of them. And the FBI knows it. The law in Chicago knows it. The press even knows it. And they don't expose the man.

And don't let me get out of here tonight without telling you why they won't expose him. Why they're afraid to expose him. They know that if they expose him, that he has them all set. See, the Black Muslim movement, it was organized in such a way that it attracted the most militant, the most uncompromising, the most fearless, and the youngest of the Black people in the United States. That's who went into it. Those who didn't mind dying. They didn't mind making a sacrifice. All they were interested in was freedom and justice and equality, and they would do anything to see that it was brought about. These are the people who have followed him for the past twelve years. And the government knows it. But all these upfront militants have been held in check by an organization that doesn't take an active part in anything. And therefore it cannot be a threat to anybody because it's not going to do anything against anybody but itself. [*Applause*]

Don't you know? The way they threw that bomb in there they could have thrown it in a Ku Klux Klan house. Why do they want to bomb my house? Why don't they bomb the Klan? I'm going to tell you why. In 1960, in

December, in December of 1960, I was in the home of
Jeremiah, the minister in Atlanta, Georgia. I'm ashamed
to say it, but I'm going to tell you the truth. I sat at the
table myself with the heads of the Ku Klux Klan. I sat
there myself, with the heads of the Ku Klux Klan, who at
that time were trying to negotiate with Elijah Muhammad so that they could make available to him a large area
of land in Georgia or I think it was South Carolina. They
had some very responsible persons in the government
who were involved in it and who were willing to go along
with it. They wanted to make this land available to him
so that his program of separation would sound more
feasible to Negroes and therefore lessen the pressure that
the integrationists were putting upon the white man. I
sat there. I negotiated it. I listened to their offer. And I
was the one who went back to Chicago and told Elijah
Muhammad what they had offered. Now, this was in
December of 1960.

The code name that Jeremiah gave the Klan leader was
666. Whenever they would refer to him they would refer
to him as Old Six. What his name was right now escapes
me. But they even sat there and told stories how—what
they had done on different escapades that they had been
involved in. Jeremiah was there and his wife was there
and I was there and the Klan was there.

From that day onward the Klan never interfered with
the Black Muslim movement in the South. Jeremiah
attended Klan rallies, as you read on the front page of the
New York Tribune. They never bothered him, never
touched him. He never touched a Muslim, and a Muslim
never touched him. Elijah Muhammad would never let
me go back down since January of 1961. I never went
South, as long as I remained in the Black Muslim movement, again, from January of 1961, because most of the
actions the Muslims got involved in was action that I was
involved in myself. Wherever it happened in the country,
where there was an action, it was action that I was

involved in, because I believed in action. I never have gone along with no Ku Klux Klan.

And another one that he had made a deal with was this man Rockwell. Rockwell and Elijah Muhammad are regular correspondents with each other. You can hate me for telling you this, but I'm going to tell it to you. Rockwell attended the rally because Elijah Muhammad put the okay on it. And Sharrieff, the captain of the FOI [Fruit of Islam], and I had discussed it, wondering why Rockwell could come to our meeting because it didn't help us. But Elijah Muhammad said let him in, so he had to be let in. No one questioned what Elijah Muhammad said. Now, if you doubt that this is true, you get all of the back issues of *Muhammad Speaks* newspaper and you will find articles in it about the Ku Klux Klan actually praising him. Jeremiah interviewed—I think it was— J.B. Stoner for the Muslim newspaper,* and the old devil even gave him a contribution that he reported about in that paper. Sure he did.

When the brothers in Monroe, Louisiana, were involved in trouble with the police, if you'll recall, Elijah Muhammad got old [James] Venable. Venable is the Ku Klux Klan lawyer. He's a Ku Klux Klan chieftain, according to the *Saturday Evening Post,* that was up on the witness stand. Go back and read the paper and you'll see that Venable was the one who represented the Black Muslim movement in Louisiana.

Now, brothers and sisters, until 1961, until 1960, until just before Elijah Muhammad went to the East, there was not a better organization among Black people in this country than the Muslim movement. It was militant. It made the whole struggle of the Black man in this country pick up momentum because of the unity, the militancy, the tendency to be uncompromising. All of these images

---

* J.B. Stoner was chairman of the National States Rights Party.

created by the Muslim movement lent weight to the struggle of the Black man in this country against oppression.

But after 1960, after Elijah Muhammad went over there in December of '59 and came back in January of '60 —when he came back, the whole trend or direction that he formerly had taken began to change. And in that change there's a whole lot of other things that had come into the picture. But he began to be more mercenary. More interested in money. More interested in wealth. And, yes, more interested in girls. [*Laughter*]

And I guess many of you have heard it said that his financial support comes from a rich man in Texas. I heard that while I was in the movement. I've heard it more since I left the movement. A rich man in Texas. You can look up, any of you can look up his name. But the FBI knows that too. But they still don't touch him. And never have I seen a man—and this rich man who lives in Texas, by the way, lives in Dallas. His headquarters is in Dallas, his money is in Dallas, the same city where President John F. Kennedy was assassinated. And never have I seen a man in my life more afraid, more frightened than Elijah Muhammad was when John F. Kennedy was assassinated. I've never in my life seen a man as frightened as he was. And when I made the statement that I did, why he almost cracked up behind it because there were all kinds of implications to it that at that time were way above and beyond my understanding.

Now you may wonder, why is it so important to many interests for the Black Muslim movement to remain? But I told you, it has the most militant, most uncompromising, most dissatisfied Black people in America in it. Many have left it, many are still in it. The fear has been that if anything happened to Elijah Muhammad and the Black Muslim movement were to crumble, that all those militants who formerly were in it and were held in check would immediately become involved in the civil rights struggle, and they would add the same kinds of energy to the civil rights struggle that they gave to the Black Muslim movement. And there's a great fear. You know yourself, white people don't like for Black people to get involved in anything to do with civil rights unless those Black people are nonviolent, loving, patient, forgiving, and all of that. They don't like it otherwise. [*Applause*]

And there has been a conspiracy across the country on the part of many factions of the press to suppress news that would open the eyes of the Muslims who are following Elijah Muhammad. They continue to make him look like he's a prophet somewhere who is getting some messages direct from God and is untouchable and things of that sort. I'm telling you the truth. But they do know that if something were to happen and all these brothers, their eyes were to come open, they would be right out here in every one of these civil rights organizations making these Uncle Tom Negro leaders stand up and fight like men instead of running around here nonviolently acting like women.

So they hope Elijah Muhammad remains as he is for a long time because they know that any organization that he heads, it will not do anything in the struggle that the Black man is confronted with in this country. Proof of which, look how violent they can get. They were violent, they've been violent from coast to coast. Muslims, in the Muslim movement, have been involved in cold, calculated violence. And not at one time have they been involved in any violence against the Ku Klux Klan. They're capable. They're qualified. They're equipped. They know how to do it. But they'll never do it—only to another brother. [*Applause*] Now, I am well aware of what I'm setting in motion by what I'm saying up here tonight. I'm well aware. But I have never said or done anything in my life that I wasn't prepared to suffer the consequences for. [*Applause*]

Now, what does this have to do with France, England,

the United States? You and I are living at a time when there's a revolution going on. A worldwide revolution. It goes beyond Mississippi. It goes beyond Alabama. It goes beyond Harlem. There's a worldwide revolution going on. And it's in two phases.

Number one, what is it revolting against? The power structure. The American power structure? No. The French power structure? No. The English power structure? No. Then what power structure? An international Western power structure. An international power structure consisting of American interests, French interests, English interests, Belgian interests, European interests. These countries that formerly colonized the dark man formed into a giant international combine. A structure, a house that has ruled the world up until now. And in recent times there has been a revolution taking place in Asia and in Africa, whacking away at the strength or at the foundation of the power structure.

Now, the man was shook up enough when Africa was in revolt and when Asia was in revolt. All of this revolt was actually taking place on the outside of his house, on the outside of his base, or on the outside of his headquarters. But now he's faced with something new. Just as the French and the British and the—the French, and the British, and the Americans formed one huge home or house or power structure, those brothers in Africa and Asia, although they are fighting against it, they also have some brothers on the inside of the house.

And as fast as the brothers in Africa and Asia get their independence, get freedom, get strength, begin to rise up, begin to change their image from negative to positive—this African image that has jumped from negative to positive affects the image that the Black man in the Western Hemisphere has of himself. Whereas in the West Indies and in Latin American countries and in the United States, you or I used to be ashamed of ourselves, used to look down upon ourselves, used to have no tendency whatsoever or desire whatsoever to stick together. As the African nations become independent and mold a new image—a positive image, a militant image, an upright image, the image of a man, not a boy—how has this affected the Black man in the Western Hemisphere? It has taken the Black man in the Caribbean and given him some pride. It has given pride to the Black man in Latin America and has given pride to the Black man right here in the United States. So that when the Black revolution begins to roll on the African continent it affects the Black man in the United States and affects the relationship between the Black man and the white man in the United States.

When the Black man in the Caribbean sees the brother on the continent of Africa waking up and rising up, the Black man in the Caribbean begins to throw back his shoulders and stick out his chest and stand up. Now, when that Black man goes to England he's right inside the English power structure, ready to give it trouble. When the Black man from the French West Indies goes to France, why the effect upon him of the African revolution is the same as the effect upon us here in the States by the African revolution. This is what you have to understand.

Now, up to now there have been Black people in France, divided. Black people in England, divided. Black people here in America, divided. What divided us? Our lack of pride. Our lack of racial identity. Our lack of racial pride. Our lack of cultural roots. We had nothing in common. But as the African nation got its independence and changed its image we became proud of it. And to the same degree that we became proud of it we began to have something in common to that same degree. So, whereas formerly it was difficult to unite Black people, today it is easier to unite Black people. Where formerly Black people didn't want to come together with Black people, but only with white people, today you find Black people want to come together with Black people. All they need is someone to start the ball rolling. . . . [*Applause*]

So this is what you have to understand. And as the brothers on the African continent lead the way, it has an effect and an impact upon the brothers here, upon the brothers here in the Western Hemisphere. So that when you find the Afro-American community in France uniting not only with itself, but for the first time beginning to unite and work in conjunction with the African community, this frightens old de Gaulle to death, because he sees some new problems in front of him.

And when the Afro—and when the West Indian community, which is an Afro-American community in England, begins to unite and then unite also with the African community in England and reach out and get the Asian community, it's trouble for old John Bull. Trouble that he never foresaw before. And this is something that he has to face up to.

Likewise, here in America, with you and me. For the first time in our history here you find we have a tendency to want to come together. For the first time we have a tendency to want to work together. And, up to now, no organization on the American continent has tried to unite you and me with our brothers and sisters back home.

At no time. None of them. [*Applause*]

Marcus Garvey did it. They put him in jail. They framed him. The government—framed him and put him in jail. Marcus Garvey tried.

The only fear that exists is that you and I once we get united will also unite with our brothers and sisters. And since they knew that my calling in life, as a Muslim—number one, I'm a Muslim, for which I'm proud. And in no way has that changed, my being a Muslim. My religion is Islam. What's that? [*Interjection from audience*] Okay. Y 'all sit down and be cool. [*Laughter*] Just sit down and be cool.

As a Muslim, when I left the Black Muslim movement, I realized that what we taught in there was not authentic

Islam. My first journey was to Mecca to make myself an authentic Muslim. And to bring them there up to date on the problems that our people who are Muslims had. As soon as we established our religious authenticity with the Muslim world, we set up the Organization of Afro-American Unity and took immediate steps to make certain that we would be in direct contact with our African brothers on the African continent.

So the first step that has been taken, brothers and sisters, since Garvey died, to actually establish contact between the 22 million Black Americans with our brothers and sisters back home was done by two organizations. Done first by the Muslim Mosque, which gave us direct ties with our brothers and sisters in Asia and Africa who are Muslims. And, you know we've got to unite with them, because there are 700 million Muslims and we surely need to stop being the minority and become part of the majority. So, as Muslims, we united with our Muslim brothers in Asia and Africa. And as members of the Organization of African, or Afro-American Unity, we set out on a program to unite our people on this continent with our people on the mother continent.

And this frightened many power—many interests in this country. Many people in this country who want to see us the minority and who don't want to see us taking too militant or too uncompromising a stand are absolutely against the successful regrouping or organizing of any faction in this country whose thought and whose thinking patterns is international, rather than national. Whose thought patterns, whose hopes and aspirations are worldly rather than just within the context of the United States border or the borderline of the United States.

So this has been the purpose of the OAAU and also the Muslim Mosque—to give us direct links, direct contact, direct communication and cooperation with our brothers and sisters all over the earth. And once we are successful in uniting ourselves with our people all over the world, it puts us in a position where we no longer are a minority who can be abused and walked upon. We become a part of the majority. And then if this man over here plays too rough, we have some brothers who can play as rough as he. [*Applause*]

So that's all I have to say about that. I wanted you to know that my house was bombed. It was bombed by the Black Muslim movement upon the orders of Elijah Muhammad. And when the bomb was thrown, one of the bombs was thrown at the rear window of my house where my three little baby girls sleep. And I have no compassion or mercy or forgiveness or anything of that sort for anyone who attacks children. If you attack me, that's one thing. I know what to do when you start attacking me, but when you attack sleeping babies, why, you are lower than a god——[*Laughter and applause*]

The only thing that I regret in all of this is that two Black groups have to fight and kill each other off. Elijah Muhammad could stop the whole thing tomorrow, just by raising his hand. Really, he could. He could stop the whole thing by raising his hand. But he won't. He doesn't love Black people. He doesn't even want to go forward. Proof of which, they're killing each other. They killed one in the Bronx. They shot another one in the Bronx. They tried to get six of us Sunday morning. And the pattern has developed across the country. The man has gone insane, absolutely out of his mind. Besides, you can't be seventy years old and surround yourself by a handful of sixteen-, seventeen-, eighteen-year-old girls and keep your right mind. [*Laughter and applause*]

So, from tonight on, there'll be a hot time in the old town [*Applause*] with regret. With great regret! There's no organization in this country that could do more for the struggling Black man than the Black Muslim movement if it wanted to, but it has gotten into the possession of a man who's become senile in his old age and perhaps doesn't realize it. And then he has surrounded himself by his children, who are now in power and want nothing but luxury and security and comfort and will do anything to safeguard their own interests.

So, I feel responsible for having played a major role in developing a criminal organization. It was not a criminal organization at the outset. It was an organization that had the power, the spiritual power, to reform the criminal. And this is what you have to understand. As long as that strong spiritual power was in the movement, it gave the moral strength to the believer that would enable him to rise above all his negative tendencies. I know, because I went into the movement with more negative tendencies than anybody in the movement. It was faith in what I was taught that made it possible for me to stop doing anything that I was doing and everything that I was doing. And I saw thousands of brothers and sisters come in who were in the same condition. And whatever they were doing, they would stop it overnight, just through faith and faith alone. And by this spiritual force, giving one the faith that enabled one to exercise some moral discipline, it became an organization that was to be respected as well as feared.

But as soon as the faith in the movement, the faith in the minds of the people in the movement was destroyed. . . . Now it has become a movement that's organized but not on a spiritual basis. And because there's no spiritual ingredient within the organization, there's no moral discipline. For it now consists of brothers and sisters who were once well meaning, but now who do not have the strength to discipline themselves. So they permit themselves to be used as a machine for a man who, as I say, has gone senile and is using them now to commit murder, acts of maiming and crippling other people.

And, I know that there's a brother sitting in here right now, tonight, who was beaten by them a couple of years ago—I'm not going to say. He knows. And if anybody should apologize to him, I should apologize to him. And I do apologize to him. Because he was beaten by the movement when I was in the movement, and I wasn't too far from him when he got beaten.

But this is what happens and this is what we have to contend with. I, for one, disassociate myself from the movement completely. And I dedicate myself to the organizing of Black people into a group that are interested in doing things constructive, not for just one religious segment of the community, but for the entire Black community. This is what the purpose of the Organization of Afro-American Unity is. To have an action program that's for the good of the entire Black community, and we are for the betterment of the community by any means necessary.

And, since tonight we had to get into this old nasty, negative subject, we didn't want to bring up our program. We're going to have a rally here this coming Sunday at two o'clock in the afternoon, at two o'clock—is it two o'clock Brother Ruben? Two o'clock. At two o'clock, at which time we will give you the program of the Organization of Afro-American Unity; what our aims are, our objectives are, what our program is, whether or not you want to be identified with it, and what active part you can play in helping us to straighten Harlem out. Nobody's going to straighten out Harlem but us. Nobody cleans up your house for you. You have to clean it up yourself. Harlem is our house; we'll clean it up. But when we clean it up, we'll also control it. We'll control the politics. We'll control the economy. We'll control the school system and see that our people get a break. [*Applause*]

So, on that note, I'm going to bring my talk to a close. I'm going to let you have a five-minute recess, during which time we're going to take up a collection so that we can pay for the expense of the hall. And then we'll take a fifteen-minute question period afterwards.

So, Brother James, is everything all set? Yes. We're going to have a—those lights are something else—we're going to have a collection period right now, and we—all we want you to do brothers and sisters, is to help us pay for the hall. And if each of you put a dollar in those white pails that's going by, we'll have the hall paid for. And I really want to apologize to you for taking your good time tonight to talk about a nasty, negative subject. But if you wake up in the middle of the night and see your house on fire all around you, with your babies crying, you'll take time to get on a nasty, negative subject, too.

QUESTIONS FROM THE PRESS

Malcolm X: I want to thank you for your patience. And ask you to be patient just a couple—this microphone doesn't seem to be up at all. Sir, was there—there was some questions you wanted to ask, was it?

[*Question unintelligible*]

Malcolm X: Yes, the press here wants to ask a couple questions. I just want to take time to answer them for them, then we'll get right into our business. We can get rid of them and get right into our business.

[*Question unintelligible*]

Malcolm X: Well, I'm not at the house, because the house was bombed out.

[*Question unintelligible*]

Malcolm X: I wouldn't say. Behind what has happened, I wouldn't ever say where I'm going to live.

Question: What do you mean when you say "there's a hot time in the old town tonight"?

Malcolm X: Well, that's an expression. Okay. . . .

This is the press. They want to get some questions out of the way. Please. When I said there'd be a hot time in the old town tonight, that's just a song, you know, that people sing. [*Laughter and applause*] Yes, sir?

[*Question unintelligible*]

Malcolm X: Yes, the house was bombed by the Black Muslim movement upon orders from Elijah Muhammad himself. And Raymond Sharrieff, the Supreme Captain of the FOI, stated in a telegram that he made public that the Muslims would not condone me making any statements about Elijah Muhammad. They let it be known where they stood and what they intended to do. And when they made such a statement, I was surprised that the police and the public didn't do something about it. But they were hoping that the Black Muslim movement could get to me and then they would move in on the Black Muslim movement. I know what they're up to. They want those fools to get me and then they'll move in on them. I can see all the way around that.

[*Question unintelligible*]

Malcolm X: Do I feel that the police—[*Interjection*]—wait a minute. Stop. Don't go anywhere. Do I feel that the New York police are providing enough protection, or do I have to have protection of my own? I look for protection from Allah.

Question: You mentioned a conspiracy between the Black Muslims and the right wing in this country. Could you elaborate?

Malcolm X: I mentioned the conspiracy between the Muslims and the right wing in this country? I know for a fact that there is a conspiracy between, among, between the Muslims and the Lincoln Rockwell Nazis and also the Ku Klux Klan. There is a conspiracy. . . . [*Interjection*]

Well, the Ku Klux Klan made a deal, or were trying to make a deal with Elijah Muhammad in 1960 in the home of Jeremiah X, the minister in Atlanta at that time, in the presence of the minister in Philadelphia. They were trying to make a deal with him to make available to Elijah Muhammad a county-size tract of land in Georgia or South Carolina where Elijah Muhammad could then induce Negroes to migrate and make it appear that his program of a segregated state or separated state was feasible. And to what extent these negotiations finally developed, I do not know. Because I was not involved in them beyond the period of December 1960. But I do know that after that, Jeremiah, who was the minister throughout the South, could roam the entire South and the Klan not bother him in any way, shape, or form, nor would they bother any of the Black Muslims from then on. Nor would the Black Muslims bother the Klan.

Question: Are you inferring because of this conspiracy the attempt was made upon your life?

Malcolm X: The attempt could have been made upon my life at the—

Question: Are you inferring that because of this conspiracy the attempt was made upon your life?

Malcolm X: Not necessarily that conspiracy. The attempt was made upon my life because I speak my mind and I know too much and they know that I will speak it—[*Applause*]

Question: Are you directing your followers to take any action?

Malcolm X: Am I directing my followers to take action against the Muslims? No. No.

[*Question unintelligible*]

Malcolm X: Am I going to try to infiltrate their organization and win over some of their supporters? No, I have never tried to win supporters from Elijah Muhammad. Since I have left the Black Muslim movement, I've spoken at these rallies. Those who come, come; those who don't, don't. But I've never gone out of my way to win over any of his followers. And he himself is fearful, because he knows that you don't have to exercise too much energy to win his followers as soon as they know the truth and compare the two—by the way, this is the brother—this is Leon Ameer, who was Cassius Clay's secretary, whom they beat unmercifully up in Boston. And the courts freed the men who beat him. They fined them $100—was it?—fined them $100 and he was on the inside of the Black Muslim specialty squad.

And it was he who heard Elijah Muhammad, Jr., come to New York when Elijah Muhammad was at the armory in June of last year. Junior stood up and told the Fruit—

many of whom are here now also—that I should have been killed. That my tongue should have been put in an envelope and sent back to Chicago by now. And because Fat Joseph had not done it, they demoted him. He remained captain, but Clarence up in Boston was put over Joseph and Joseph's authority was curtailed. And then Clarence, the captain from Boston, and John, the captain from Springfield, came to New York to assassinate me. And came to him to get a silencer and couldn't get it. So the police know this. It's not something that's new. They're just waiting until the job is done and then they step in.

Question: Do you know that Elijah Muhammad was behind this?

Malcolm X: Yes.

Question: Or is this your belief?

Malcolm X: Elijah Muhammad invited—called all of his officials, national officials, to Chicago in October and ordered them to kill or maim any of his followers who leave him to follow me.

[*Question unintelligible*]

Malcolm X: Well, when you say, how do I know. Many of the brothers who were in at that time are out now. And if this ever comes into the courts, there are plenty of witnesses who can stand up and testify to it.

[*Question unintelligible*]

Malcolm X: I'd rather not say at this time.

[*Question unintelligible, protests from audience*]

Malcolm X: Give them two more minutes and we'll end it.

[*Question unintelligible*]

Malcolm X: Yes, when I said that no one could clean up our homes but us, and that we will clean it up and that no one should control it but us, including the politics; what do I mean? I mean exactly that. That the Black people—[*Interjection*] What? Including who? Powell? [Congressman Adam Clayton] Powell is one of us—[*Applause*]

[*Question unintelligible*]

Malcolm X: No, he's not a member of our organization, but when I say he is one of us I mean he's one of the family. And then no one outside the family can get up and talk about him. If we talk about him, we talk about him within the family. But nobody outside the family can instigate us against Powell. [*Applause*]

[*Question unintelligible*]

Malcolm X: Yes, by controlling it politically I mean that the politics of the community of Harlem should be controlled by those of us who live in Harlem. Not by somebody sitting down in Gracie Mansion.* [*Applause*]

[*Question unintelligible*]

Malcolm X: No. But the Organization of Afro-American Unity intends to get involved in every kind of action that's going on in New York City. We don't intend to let anybody downtown influence us in any way, shape, or form. We want the influence to come from Harlem. And from other Harlems around the country. Now, this doesn't mean we're anti-outside of Harlem. This doesn't mean we're anti-Bronx or anti–White Plains or antiwhite or anti-German or anything like that. But it means we're pro-Harlem. We're pro-ourselves. We want to start doing something for ourselves. That's all it means. It means that we want to stop begging you for your school; we want you to get out of the way and let us straighten out the schools in Harlem. [*Applause*]

[*Question unintelligible*]

Malcolm X: I just answered this when I said from tonight on there will be a hot time in the old town. I answered it when this gentleman over here asked. The song will be the same. [*Interjection*] An implication? [*Interjection*] An implied threat? I never imply any threat to

---

* Gracie Mansion is the official residence of the mayor of New York City.

anyone. I am a Muslim, my religion is Islam—it's a religion of peace.

Question: Do you think there will be any further attempts?

Malcolm X: Sir, yes I do believe there will be further attempts on my life. I know them. They are foaming at the mouth. The rank-and-file Muslim means well. It's those at the hierarchy, who are living off the fatted calf, who don't mean well. And this coming Sunday at two o'clock, as I say, our program will be unfolded.

Elijah Muhammad knows—he has done some good things and he has done some bad things. He knows that if he had wanted to, he could have united our people with the Muslim world just by teaching the right religion of Islam. He could have done so. The entire Muslim world would have accepted him; as it is now, the Muslim world has rejected him. He can never go into the Muslim world and say that he is a prophet or that Allah came over here in the flesh—they would cut his head off if he said that. I mean he knows this. None of his followers can go over there without denouncing him. It is impossible for them to go to Mecca or any other place unless they subscribe to Islam, as it is subscribed to over there. So he was in a position to unite us with the Muslim world, those of us who were Muslim. He was also in a position to unite us with Africa. But you cannot read anything that Elijah Muhammad has ever written that's pro-African. I defy you to find one word in his direct writings that's pro-African. You can't find it.

[*Question unintelligible*]

Malcolm X: Listen to this question this man got. What are you trying to get at?

[*Question unintelligible*]

Malcolm X: No, he asked me. No. I got to tell them what you asked me. He asked me, don't I think if I got hurt, you know, wouldn't some of my followers retaliate? What are you trying to say? [*Laughter*] Or, what are you trying to get me to say? [*Laughter*]

No. I mean, it's okay. I'm not going to get you into any trouble. These are your friends in here. [*Laughter*] I just want them to hear what you're asking me. That's all. [*Laughter*] I just want them to hear what you're asking me. You're not going to get in no trouble for this. Would he? [*Laughter*] No.

Yes sir, last question.

Question: You're under civil court order to get out of your house in Queens—

Malcolm X: I'm under a civil court order to get out of my house in Queens? You know, I only—somebody told that they heard that on the radio. I know nothing about it. And I haven't discussed it with a lawyer yet and I won't make any comments until I've discussed it with a lawyer. But I just hope that nobody tries to go in there while what's left of my belongings are there.

[*Question unintelligible*]

Malcolm X: Some have been in the vicinity, yes, and some policemen, too, have been nice enough to watch the house ever since it was bombed. I wish they had been watching it while it was bombed.

[*Question unintelligible*]

Malcolm X: Yeah, a great deal of my personal belongings were lost. They threw four bombs in there. I might point this out, that those who did it were so vicious and those who did it knew the whole layout of the house. They—and to show you why I believe in Allah—the bombs that were thrown into the front part of the house were thrown directly against the window, you know, so they came through. But before they threw the first one, the neighbors saw someone go up to the window with a moplike instrument and break the windows, crack the glass, and then they threw the bombs in after the glass was broken and that was in the front part.

Now if they had come around to the—they had planned to do it from the front and the back so that I couldn't get out. They covered the front completely, the front door. Then they had come to the back but instead of getting directly in back of the house and throwing it this way, they stood at a forty-five degree angle and tossed it at the window so it glanced and went onto the ground. And the fire hit the window and it woke up my second oldest baby, but the fire burned on the outside of the house. But had that fire, had that gone through that window it would have fallen on a six-year-old girl, a four-year-old girl, and a two-year-old girl.

Now I'm going to tell you, if it had done it I'd taken my rifle and gone after anybody in sight. I would not wait. I say that because of this. The police know the criminal operation of the Black Muslim movement because they have thoroughly infiltrated it. There is no conversation that takes place in the Black Muslim movement that the city police don't know about, because they have policemen in there. They don't let Black people form anything without some policemen in there. And while I was in the Black Muslim movement, over the Black Muslim movement, many of the police who were sent to infiltrate us—they're Black—would tell me, "Look, I'm a cop, but I have to come." They would tell me. I knew the Muslim movement was full of police. So don't you think anything is going down that they don't know about. The only thing that goes down is what they want to go down, and what they don't want to go down they don't let it go down.

Question: I have one last question.

Malcolm X: One last question, yes sir.

Question: The Muslims claim that you bombed your own house.

Malcolm X: Yes, that's what I said. The Muslims claim I bombed my house.

Question: Of course, they say, while you were there.

Malcolm X: Yeah. No, well, you can think what you want. The arson squad, the fire marshal, all of them are experts in this kind of thing. And if anybody can find where I've bombed my house, they can put a rifle bullet through my head. It was my children and my own life and my wife's life that was at stake.

Hey, let me tell you something, sir. I stood Sunday morning, you know what the degree—what the temperature was? It was about fifteen or twenty. I stood in my underwear, barefeet in the middle of my driveway with a gun in my hands for forty-five minutes waiting for the police or waiting for the fire department to come. If I'd wanted to put on a show I could find a better way than that to put it on. [*Applause*]

That's all.

DISCUSSION PERIOD

Malcolm X: There's a—brothers and sisters, there's a—here's the *Saturday Evening Post* dated February 27, 1965, and in it there's an article titled, "An ex-official tells why the Black Muslims are a fraud." This is one of the brothers in Boston and who was formerly the secretary up there and who is the cousin of Ronald Stokes, the brother who was killed out in California in April of 1962.[*] And I would like to say this before anything else, and that is don't think that I don't know how bad I make myself look by attacking an organization that I was once so inseparably a part of. Well, I'm not particularly concerned with how bad it makes me look. My prime concern is to expose it to the fullest of my ability, let the chips fall where they may. [*Applause*]

And if the Black Muslim movement says that I'm wrong in what I say, then I say since they're so well qualified and equipped, let them attack the Klan. Let them go find out who—let them get the persons who bombed that church in Birmingham. Because I'll go get them. I'll go attack the Klan. And attack Rockwell and any of the

---

* Muslim Ronald X Stokes was shot by police during an April 1962 melee outside the Los Angeles temple.

others. And I defy them to do so. They can't do it. Because they both have the same paymaster. [*Applause*]

So now our question period. And you have to stand up because I can't see beyond this man's light.

Yes sir.

[*Question unintelligible*]

Malcolm X: Don't I think that we should become involved in some direct action, demonstrations? We are going to unveil our program on that next Sunday at two o'clock. Brother, I'm for anything you're for as long as it's going to get some results. I'm for anything you're for. [*Applause*] As long as it's intelligent, as long as it's disciplined, as long as it's aimed in the right direction—I'm for it.

And what determines what we should do, or shouldn't do, will in no way be influenced by what the man downtown thinks. We don't need anybody on the outside laying the ground rules by which we are going to fight our battles. We'll study the battle, study the enemy, study what we're up against, and then outline or map our own battle strategy. And we'll get some results. But as long as you have someone coming in from the outside telling you how you should do it and how you shouldn't do it—and always what they tell you is nonviolence, peaceful, love everybody, forgive them Lord, they know not what they do. As long as you get into that kind of bag, why you'll never get anywhere.

What we want is to let them know that our aims are just. Our aims are within the realm of justice. And since they are, we're justified in going after those aims.

Don't you know it's a disgrace for the United States of America to let—to have Martin Luther King, my good friend, the Right Reverend Dr. Martin, in Alabama, using school children to do what the federal government should do. Think of this. Those school children shouldn't have to march. Why Lyndon Johnson is supposed to have troops down there marching. Your children aren't supposed to have to get out there and demonstrate just to vote. Is it that bad? It shows our so-called leaders have been out-maneuvered.

Every day, you look on the television, you listen to the radio, you read the newspaper, and see where Black people are going to jail by the hundreds, by the thousands. You don't do this in a civilized country. In any other country, the government would do its job. But this exists only because the government is not doing its job. They've got Martin Luther King down there with crocodile tears crying his way into jail and still coming out and haven't got the ballot yet. We can get the ballot. [*Applause*]

Didn't they pass the civil rights bill? Just a minute, didn't they pass the civil rights bill and have made it legal. Don't you know that anywhere our people want to register and vote they're within their legal rights? All you and I have to do is show that we're men. And when we, and when they go to vote, we go with them. With them. With them. Prepared! [*Applause*]

Not prepared to make trouble. Not prepared to cause trouble. But prepared to protect ourselves in case trouble comes our way. [*Applause*] And no one can find fault with that. Yes ma'am?

Question: My nephew is in Vietnam and—

Malcolm X: Your nephew is where?

Question: In South Vietnam—

Malcolm X: In Vietnam? You should have him in Alabama.

[*Question unintelligible*]

Malcolm X: You told him right. [*Applause*] Sister, you're talking my kind of talk. Yeah.

[*Question unintelligible*]

Malcolm X: I know you would. I know you would. [*Applause*] Who else? Yes ma'am? . . .

Question: Brother Malcolm [*Unintelligible*] have fallen out of a hospital window. We buried him Saturday. [*Unintelligible*] refuse to speak to anyone. They have not spoken to his mother or anyone else. We have sent delegations there and each time they tell us that there's no one available to speak to. I had a picket line there Saturday. . . . Now can't something be done about this? A thirteen-year-old child?

Malcolm X: Fell out of the hospital window?

Question: So they say. But this child had lived on the top floor all of his life. . . . What can we do and what must we do to avoid something else like this?

Malcolm X: This is what I meant earlier when I said concerning the importance of our controlling Harlem. As long as we have outsiders running our hospitals and our schools and our everything else, they will run us right on out of existence. I would suggest that you come over to the office and see what we can get our heads together on. And see what we can do. Anything I can do, I certainly will and I know all the brothers and sisters will. [Applause]

We have time for two more questions. Yes ma'am. Right in front.

[*Question unintelligible*]

Malcolm X: No, they're not. They're marching for their parents. Let me tell you. You know, I was in Selma, and when I got to Selma I talked to these children.* I talked to them. And you know I have to say this. I have to expose the man. King's man did not want me to talk to them. They told me they didn't mind me coming in and all of that but they preferred that I didn't talk to the children. Because they knew what I was going to say. [*Laughter*] But the children insisted that I be heard. Otherwise, I wouldn't have gotten a hearing at all. And some of the,

---

* Despite civil rights legislation, in early 1965 most Blacks in Selma, Alabama, were still denied the right to vote. Massive demonstrations there, beginning in January, received wide national attention as Sheriff Jim Clark led a campaign of violent attacks on demonstrators. Selma became synonymous with violent racist reaction to the civil rights movement.

many of the students from SNCC [Student Nonviolent Coordinating Committee] also insisted that I be heard. This is the only way I got a chance to talk to them.

And I might point out that one little girl who was only thirteen years old told me that she had been in jail the night before. She had just gotten out that morning. And she told of how they were using cattle prods, sticking it up against the heads of some of these little children and giving them headaches and things of that sort.

Oh, yes. The most brutal form of punishment imaginable takes place down there and nothing is done about it. Old Lyndon is all tied up in South Vietnam and the Congo and other places, but he's not minding his business in Mississippi, in Alabama.

But you see, I don't blame them. I blame us. Really, I blame us. Once we organize, we can straighten it out. The government is not going to straighten it out. It's getting too corrupt. It has too many racists in it. Too many segregationists running the government. So how is somebody from Texas going to stop the Klan? From Texas! Texas is a Klan state itself. No. . . . You and I have to do it.

And I promised the brothers and sisters in Alabama when I was there that we'd be back. I'll be back, you'll be back, we'll be back. We'll ease on in, brothers and sisters. [*Applause*]

Those people down there aren't afraid. They aren't afraid, they're just waiting for somebody to tell them what to do. That's all. And they don't go for that old turn-the-other-cheek stuff. No. That's why they got children doing it. And even those children don't go for turning the other cheek. And there's nothing wrong with my saying this.

Any time you live in a government, a government in 1965, that will permit conditions to exist that force a Negro leader to take children—babies—and march them down the street to get the right to register and vote, why that government should come under question. Should come under examination. We should stop and take a second look at it. And if it's not the government, then it's the men in the government. But the blame has got to be put somewhere. But you know where I put it? On us. We're too easy. We're too forgiving. We're too loving. We're too forgetful. We're too compromising. And we're too peaceful. Time for one more question. Yes sir. . . . Yes, yes ma'am.

[*Question unintelligible*]

Malcolm X: Yes, Yes. Akbar Muhammad along with Wallace Muhammad. But Akbar Muhammad gave a press conference in Cairo completely disassociating himself from his father and pointing out that what Elijah Muhammad is teaching in this country is absolutely and diametrically opposed to the true teachings of Islam. This was in Cairo.

And actually what Elijah Muhammad is teaching is an insult to the entire Muslim world, because Islam as the religion, as a religion, has nothing to do with color. There is no religion that has anything to do with color and Islam—as a religion, it doesn't use the color of a man's skin to measure him or as a yardstick. Islam, as a religion, judges a man by his intention, by his behavior, by his deeds. Now I can judge these crackers not 'cause they're white—I'm not talking about them 'cause they're white. I'm talking about them 'cause what they do. Do you understand? Anything you hear me say here about whitey, or the white man, is not because he's white—no, I'll shake his hand if he's all right. But first he got to get all right. [*Laughter and applause*]

The standard of judgment from a Muslim is behavior, intention, and deed. Do you understand? What Elijah Muhammad teaches is not that. Yes sir.

Question: Getting back to the action.

Malcolm X: The action, yes.

Question: You know, having power, wouldn't it be better if we were—I mean speaking of the Black man—to form a Black Ku Klux Klan?

Malcolm X: No. No. No. Don't let them maneuver you into forming anything that can be compared with the Klan. See, it is true we're the target of brutal, criminal treatment from the Klan. Now, we don't need a Black Ku Klux Klan. All we need is Black people who believe in the brotherhood of man and who will fight anyone who threatens the brotherhood of man. Now, the Klan is a threat to this brotherhood and we are legally within our rights to defend ourselves from this Klan.

But if we call ourselves the Klan, what will happen— the press will pick up what you do and make what you do look wrong. Because they will make it look wrong anyway. So if you call yourself that, you help them. You help them hurt you. No we don't want anything to do with the Klan or anything like the Klan. We want to destroy the Klan. Disband it, destroy it, erase it from this earth. And we can do it. You've been in the army. They taught you all those tricks. [*Laughter*] Well, use them. [*Laughter and applause*]

I got to say this; then we're going to close. You need to study guerrilla warfare. Get every book you can find on guerrilla warfare. [*Laughter*] There's nothing wrong with saying that. Yes, it's good to know everything. There's nothing wrong with knowing that. Why, the government teaches you that. [*Laughter*]

They draft you to teach you that, don't they? Sure, they taught it to your son. Well, go on and teach it to your son. But then tell your son how to use it. [*Applause and laughter*]

No, you study. We're going to have classes. The OAAU is going to have classes in all of the various sciences that you and I need to know—karate, judo. We've got some experts. This brother here is an expert judo man, expert karate man. He'd break that board right here like it wasn't even a board. You come on in the OAAU and we'll train you. Show you how to protect yourself. Not so that you can go out and attack someone. You should never attack anybody. But at the same time whenever you, yourself, are attacked you are not supposed to turn the other cheek. Never turn the other cheek until you see the white man turn his cheek. The day that the white man turns the cheek, then you turn the cheek. If Martin Luther King was teaching white people to turn the other cheek, then I would say he was justified in teaching Black people to turn the other cheek. That's all I'm against. Make it a two-way street. Make it even steven. If I'm going to be nonviolent, then let them be nonviolent. But as long as they're not nonviolent, don't you let anybody tell you anything about nonviolence. No. Be intelligent.

Brothers and sisters, we're going to have our program on Sunday at two o'clock. I hope that every one of you will be here. It will be one of the last programs that we have—please don't move; please don't move; please don't move. It's going to be one of the last programs we have. Next Sunday, at two o'clock. It will be designed to unfold to you completely, what our program is, and as I said earlier—some of you came late—the only reason that I didn't do it tonight, I wanted to give you a complete clarification on what happened at my house Sunday morning, so that you would know. And once you know, then you can stay way away from me or come on in, we'll get you, one of the two. But I don't want to get you into anything that you don't know what you're getting into. I'm not trying to get you in any trouble, but I am trying to get something organized that will enable us to take a direct action against the forces that have been holding us back. Now they asked me to—Brother Benjamin will tell you what else there is in just two minutes while there's something else I have to do.

Not just an American problem, but a world problem

FIRST, brothers and sisters, I want to start by thanking you for taking the time to come out this evening and especially for the invitation for me to come up to Rochester and participate in this little informal discussion this evening on matters that are of common interest to all elements in the community, in the entire Rochester community. My reason for being here is to discuss the Black revolution that is going on, that's taking place on this earth, the manner in which it's taking place on the African continent, and the impact that it's having in Black communities, not only here in America but in England and in France and in other of the former colonial powers today.

Many of you probably read last week I made an effort to go to Paris and was turned away. And Paris doesn't turn anybody away. You know anybody is supposed to be able to go to France, it's supposed to be a very liberal place. But France is having problems today that haven't been highly publicized. And England is also having problems that haven't been highly publicized, because America's problems have been so highly publicized. But all of these three partners, or allies, have troubles in common today that the Black American, or Afro-American, isn't well enough up on.

And in order for you and me to know the nature of the struggle that you and I are involved in, we have to know not only the various ingredients involved at the local level and national level, but also the ingredients that are involved at the international level. And the problems of the Black man here in this country today have ceased to be a problem of just the American Negro or an American problem. It has become a problem that is so complex, and has so many implications in it, that you have to study it in its entire world, in the world context or in its international context, to really see it as it actually is. Otherwise you can't even follow the local issue, unless you know what part it plays in the entire international context. And when you look at it in that context, you see it in a different light, but you see it with more clarity.

And you should ask yourself why should a country like France be so concerned with a little insignificant American Negro that they would prohibit him from going there, when almost anybody else can go to that country whenever they desire. And it's primarily because the three countries have the same problems. And the problem is this: That in the Western Hemisphere, you and I haven't realized it, but we aren't exactly a minority on this earth. In the Western Hemisphere there are—there's the people in Brazil, two-thirds of the people in Brazil are dark-skinned people, the same as you and I. They are people of African origin, African ancestry—African background. And not only in Brazil, but throughout Latin America, the Caribbean, the United States, and Canada, you have people here who are of African origin.

Many of us fool ourselves into thinking of Afro-Americans as those only who are here in the United States. America is North America, Central America, and South America. Anybody of African ancestry in South America is an Afro-American. Anybody in Central America of African blood is an Afro-American. Anybody here in North America, including Canada, is an Afro-American if he has African ancestry—even down in the Caribbean, he's an Afro-American. So when I speak of the Afro-American, I'm not speaking of just the 22 million of us who are here in the United States. But the Afro-American is that large number of people in the Western Hemisphere, from the southernmost tip of South America to the northernmost tip of North America, all of whom have a common heritage and have a common origin when you go back to the roots of these people.

Now, there are four spheres of influence in the Western Hemisphere, where Black people are concerned. There's the Spanish influence, which means that Spain formerly colonized a certain area of the Western Hemisphere. There's the French sphere of influence, which means that area that she formerly colonized. The area that the British formerly colonized. And then those of us who are in the United States.

The area that was formerly colonized by the Spanish is commonly referred to as Latin America. They have many dark-skinned people there, of African ancestry. The area which the French colonized here in the Western Hemisphere is largely referred to as the French West Indies. And the area that the British colonized are those that are commonly referred to as the British West Indies, and also Canada. And then again, there's the United States. So we have these four different classifications of Black people, or nonwhite people, here in the Western Hemisphere.

Because of the poor economy of Spain, and because it has ceased to be an influence on the world scene as it formerly was, not very many of the people from—not very many of the black-skinned people from the Spanish sphere of influence migrate to Spain. But because of the high standard of living in France and England, you find many of the Black people from the British West Indies have been migrating to Great Britain, many of the Black people from the French West Indies migrate to France, and then you and I are already here.

So it means that the three major allies, the United States, Britain, and France, have a problem today that is a common problem. But you and I are never given enough information to realize that they have a common problem. And that common problem is the new mood that is reflected in the overall division of the Black people within continental France, within the same sphere of England, and also here in the United States. So that—and this mood has been changing to the same degree that the mood on the African continent has been changing. So when you find the African revolution taking place, and by African revolution I mean the emergence of African nations into independence that has been going on for the past ten or twelve years, has absolutely affected the mood of the Black people in the Western Hemisphere. So much so that when they migrate to England, they pose a problem for the English. And when they migrate to France, they pose a problem for the French. And when they—already here in the States—but when they awaken, and this same mood is reflected in the Black man in the States, then it poses a problem to the white man here in America.

And don't you think that the problem that the white man in America has is unique. France is having the same problem. And Great Britain is having the same problem. But the only difference between the problem in France and Britain and here is there have been many Black leaders that have risen up here in the Western Hemisphere, in the United States, that have created so much sort of militancy that has frightened the American whites. But that has been absent in France and England. And it has only been recently that the American Negro community and the British West Indian community, along with the African community in France, have begun to organize among themselves, and it's frightening France to death. And the same thing is happening in England. It is—up until recently it was disorganized completely. But recently, the West Indians in England, along with the African community in England, along with the Asians in England began to organize and work in coordination with each other, in conjunction with each other. And this has posed England a very serious problem.

So I had to give you that background, in order for you to understand some of the current problems that are developing here on this earth. And in no time can you understand the problems between Black and white people here in Rochester or Black and white people in Mississippi or Black and white people in California, unless you understand the basic problem that exists between Black and white people—not confined to the local level, but confined to the international, global level on this earth today. When you look at it in that context, you'll understand. But if you only try to look at it in the local context, you'll never understand. You have to see the trend that is taking place on this earth. And my purpose for coming here tonight is to try and give you as up-to-date an understanding of it all as is possible.

As many of you know, I left the Black Muslim movement and during the summer months, I spent five of those months on the—in the Middle East and on the African continent. During this time I visited many countries, first of which was Egypt, and then Arabia, then Kuwait, Lebanon, Sudan, Kenya, Ethiopia, Zanzibar, Tanganyika—which is now Tanzania—Nigeria, Ghana, Guinea, Liberia, Algeria. And then the five months that I was away I had an opportunity to hold lengthy discussions with President Nasser in Egypt, President Julius Nyerere in Tanzania, Jomo Kenyatta in Kenya, Milton Obote in Uganda, Azikiwe in Nigeria, Nkrumah in Ghana, and Sékou Touré in Guinea.

And during conversations with these men, and other Africans on that continent, there was much information exchanged that definitely broadened my understanding, and I feel, broadened my scope. For since coming back from over there, I have had no desire whatsoever to get bogged down in any picayune arguments with any bird-brained or small-minded people who happen to belong to organizations, based upon facts that are very misleading and don't get you anywhere when you have problems as complex as ours that are trying to get solved.

So I'm not here tonight to talk about some of these movements that are clashing with each other. I'm here to talk about the problem that's in front of all of us. And to have—and to do it in a very informal way. I never like to be tied down to a formal method or procedure when talking to an audience, because I find that usually the conversation that I'm involved in revolves around race, or things racial, which is not my fault. I didn't create the race problem. And you know, I didn't come to America on the *Mayflower* or at my own volition. Our people were brought here involuntarily, against our will. So if we pose the problem now, they shouldn't blame us for being here. They brought us here.

[*Applause*]

One of the reasons I feel that it is best to remain very informal when discussing this type of topic, when people are discussing things based on race, they have a tendency to be very narrow-minded and to get emotional and all involved in—especially white people. I have found white people that usually are very intelligent, until you get them to talking about the race problem. Then they get blind as a bat and want you to see what they know is the exact opposite of the truth. [*Applause*]

So what I would rather we try and do is be very informal, where we can relax and keep an open mind, and try and form the pattern or the habit of seeing for ourselves, hearing for ourselves, thinking for ourselves, and then we can come to an intelligent judgment for ourselves.

To straighten out my own position, as I did earlier in the day at Colgate, I'm a Muslim, which only means that my religion is Islam. I believe in God, the Supreme Being, the creator of the universe. This is a very simple form of religion, easy to understand. I believe in one God. It's just a whole lot better. But I believe in one God, and I believe that that God had one religion, has one religion, always will have one religion. And that that God taught all of the prophets the same religion, so there is no argument about who was greater or who was better: Moses, Jesus, Muhammad, or some of the others. All of them were prophets who came from one God. They had one doctrine, and that doctrine was designed to give clarification of humanity, so that all of humanity would see that it was one and have some kind of brotherhood that would be practiced here on this earth. I believe in that.

I believe in the brotherhood of man. But despite the fact that I believe in the brotherhood of man, I have to be a realist and realize that here in America we're in a society that doesn't practice brotherhood. It doesn't practice what it preaches. It preaches brotherhood, but it doesn't practice brotherhood. And because this society doesn't practice brotherhood, those of us who are Muslim—those of us who left the Black Muslim movement and regrouped as Muslims, in a movement based upon orthodox Islam—we believe in the brotherhood of Islam.

But we also realize that the problem facing Black people in this country is so complex and so involved and has been here so long, unsolved, that it is absolutely necessary for us to form another organization. Which we did, which is a nonreligious organization in which—is known as the Organization of Afro-American Unity, and it is so structured organizationally to allow for active participation of any Afro-American, any Black American, in a program that is designed to eliminate the negative political, economic, and social evils that our people are confronted by in this society. And we have that set up because we realize that we have to fight against the evils of a society that has failed to produce brotherhood for every member of that society. This in no way means that we're antiwhite, antiblue, antigreen, or antiyellow. We're antiwrong. We're antidiscrimination. We're antisegregation. We're against anybody who wants to practice some form of segregation or discrimination against us because we don't happen to be a color that's acceptable to you. . . . [*Applause*]

We don't judge a man because of the color of his skin. We don't judge you because you're white; we don't judge you because you're black; we don't judge you because you're brown. We judge you because of what you do and what you practice. And as long as you practice evil, we're against you. And for us, the most—the worst form of evil is the evil that's based upon judging a man because of the color of his skin. And I don't think anybody here can deny that we're living in a society that just doesn't judge a man according to his talents, according to his know-how, according to his possibility—background, or lack of academic background. This society judges a man solely upon the color of his skin. If you're white, you can go forward, and if you're Black, you have to fight your way every step of the way, and you still don't get forward. [*Applause*]

We are living in a society that is by and large controlled by people who believe in segregation. We are living in a society that is by and large controlled by a people who believe in racism, and practice segregation and discrimination and racism. We believe in a—and I say that it is controlled, not by the well-meaning whites, but controlled by the segregationists, the racists. And you can see by the pattern that this society follows all over the world. Right now in Asia you have the American army dropping bombs on dark-skinned people. You can't say that—it's as though you can justify being that far from home, dropping bombs on somebody else. If you were next door, I could see it, but you can't go that far away from this country and drop bombs on somebody else and justify your presence over there, not with me. [*Applause*]

It's racism. Racism practiced by America. Racism which involves a war against the dark-skinned people in Asia, another form of racism involving a war against the dark-skinned people in the Congo* ... as it involves a war against the dark-skinned people in Mississippi, Alabama, Georgia, and Rochester, New York. [*Applause*]

So we're not against people because they're white. But we're against those who practice racism. We're against those who drop bombs on people because their color happens to be of a different shade than yours. And because we're against it, the press says we're violent. We're not for violence. We're for peace. But the people that we're up against are for violence. You can't be peaceful when you're dealing with them. [*Applause*]

They accuse us of what they themselves are guilty of. This is what the criminal always does. They'll bomb you, then accuse you of bombing yourself. They'll crush your skull, then accuse you of attacking him. This is what the racists have always done—the criminal, the one who has criminal processes developed to a science. Their practice is criminal action. And then use the press to make you victim—look like the victim is the criminal, and the criminal is the victim. This is how they do it. [*Applause*]

And you here in Rochester probably know more about this than anybody anywhere else. Here's an example of how they do. They take the press, and through the press, they beat the system. ... Or through the white public. Because the white public is divided. Some mean good, and some don't mean good. Some are well meaning, and some are not well meaning. This is true. You got some that are not well meaning, and some are well meaning. And usually those that are not well meaning outnumber those that are well meaning. You need a microscope to find those that are well meaning. [*Applause*]

So they don't like to do anything without the support of

---

* See footnote on page 92.

the white public. The racists, that are usually very influential in the society, don't make their move without first going to get public opinion on their side. So they use the press to get public opinion on their side. When they want to suppress and oppress the Black community, what do they do? They take the statistics, and through the press, they feed them to the public. They make it appear that the role of crime in the Black community is higher than it is anywhere else.

What does this do? [*Applause*] This message—this is a very skillful message used by racists to make the whites who aren't racists think that the rate of crime in the Black community is so high. This keeps the Black community in the image of a criminal. It makes it appear that anyone in the Black community is a criminal. And as soon as this impression is given, then it makes it possible, or paves the way to set up a police-type state in the Black community, getting the full approval of the white public when the police come in, use all kind of brutal measures to suppress Black people, crush their skulls, sic dogs on them, and things of that type. And the whites go along with it. Because they think that everybody over there's a criminal anyway. This is what—the press does this. [*Applause*]

This is skill. This skill is called—this is a science that's called "image making." They hold you in check through this science of imagery. They even make you look down upon yourself, by giving you a bad image of yourself. Some of our own Black people who have eaten this image themselves and digested it—until they themselves don't want to live in the Black community. They don't want to be around Black people themselves. [*Applause*]

It's a science that they use, very skillfully, to make the criminal look like the victim, and to make the victim look like the criminal. Example: In the United States during the Harlem riots, I was in Africa, fortunately. [*Laughter*] During these riots, or because of these riots, or after the riots, again the press, very skillfully, depicted the rioters as hoodlums, criminals, thieves, because they were abducting some property.

Now mind you, it is true that property was destroyed. But look at it from another angle. In these Black communities, the economy of the community is not in the hands of the Black man. The Black man is not his own landlord. The buildings that he lives in are owned by someone else. The stores in the community are run by someone else. Everything in the community is out of his hands. He has no say-so in it whatsoever, other than to live there, and pay the highest rent for the lowest-type boarding place, [*Applause*] pays the highest prices for food, for the lowest grade of food. He is a victim of this, a victim of economic exploitation, political exploitation, and every other kind.

Now, he's so frustrated, so pent-up, so much explosive energy within him, that he would like to get at the one who's exploiting him. But the one who's exploiting him doesn't live in his neighborhood. He only owns the house. He only owns the store. He only owns the neighborhood. So that when the Black man explodes, the one that he wants to get at isn't there. So he destroys the property. He's not a thief. He's not trying to steal your cheap furniture or your cheap food. He wants to get at you, but you're not there. [*Applause*]

And instead of the sociologists analyzing it as it actually is, trying to understand it as it actually is, again they cover up the real issue, and they use the press to make it appear that these people are thieves, hoodlums. No! They are the victims of organized thievery, organized landlords who are nothing but thieves, merchants who are nothing but thieves, politicians who sit in the city hall and who are nothing but thieves in cahoots with the landlords and the merchants. [*Applause*]

But again, the press is used to make the victim look like the criminal and make the criminal look like the victim. . . . This is imagery. And just as this imagery is practiced at the local level, you can understand it better by an international example. The best recent example at the international level to bear witness to what I'm saying is what happened in the Congo. Look at what happened. We had a situation where a plane was dropping bombs on African villages. An African village has no defense against the bombs. And an African village is not sufficient threat that it has to be bombed! But planes were dropping bombs on African villages. When these bombs strike, they don't distinguish between enemy and friend. They don't distinguish between male and female. When these bombs are dropped on African villages in the Congo, they are dropped on Black women, Black children, Black babies. These human beings were blown to bits. I heard no outcry, no voice of compassion for these thousands of Black people who were slaughtered by planes. [*Applause*]

Why was there no outcry? Why was there no concern? Because, again, the press very skillfully made the victims look like they were the criminals, and the criminals look like they were the victims. [*Applause*]

They refer to the villages as "rebel held," you know. As if to say, because they are rebel-held villages, you can destroy the population, and it's okay. They also refer to the merchants of death as "American-trained, anti-Castro Cuban pilots." This made it okay. Because these pilots, these mercenaries—you know what a mercenary is, he's not a patriot. A mercenary is not someone who goes to war out of patriotism for his country. A mercenary is a hired killer. A person who kills, who draws blood for money, anybody's blood. You kill a human being as easily as you kill a cat or a dog or a chicken.

So these mercenaries, dropping bombs on African villages, caring nothing as to whether or not there are innocent, defenseless women and children and babies being destroyed by their bombs. But because they're called "mercenaries," given a glorified name, it doesn't excite you. Because they are referred to as "American-trained" pilots, because they are American-trained, that makes them okay. "Anti-Castro Cubans," that makes them okay. Castro's a monster, so anybody who's against Castro is all right with us, and anything they can do from there, that's all right with us. . . . They put your mind right in a bag and take it wherever they want, as well. [*Applause*]

But it's something that you have to look at and answer for. Because they are American planes, American bombs, escorted by American paratroopers, armed with machine guns. But, you know, they say they're not soldiers, they're just there as escorts, like they started out with some advisers in South Vietnam. Twenty thousand of them— just advisers. These are just "escorts." They're able to do all of this mass murder and get away with it by labeling it "humanitarian," an act of humanitarianism. Or "in the name of freedom," "in the name of liberty." All kinds of high-sounding slogans, but it's cold-blooded murder, mass murder. And it's done so skillfully, so you and I, who call ourselves sophisticated in this twentieth century, are able to watch it, and put the stamp of approval upon it. Simply because it's being done to people with black skin, by people with white skin.

They take a man who is a cold-blooded murderer, named [Moise] Tshombe. You've heard of him, Uncle Tom Tshombe. [*Laughter and applause*] He murdered the prime minister, the rightful prime minister, [Patrice] Lumumba. He murdered him. [*Applause*] Now here's a man who's an international murderer, selected by the State Department and placed over the Congo and propped into position by your tax dollars. He's a killer. He's hired by our government. He's a hired killer. And to show the type of hired killer he is, as soon as he's in office, he hires more killers in South Africa to shoot down his own people. And you wonder why your American image abroad is so bankrupt.

Notice I said, "Your American image abroad is so bankrupt."

They make this man acceptable by saying in the press that he's the only one that can unite the Congo. Ha. A murderer. They won't let China in the United Nations because they say she declared war on UN troops in Korea. Tshombe declared war on UN troops in Katanga. You give him money and prop him up. You don't use the same yardstick. You use the yardstick over here, change it over here.

This is true—everybody can see you today. You make yourself look sick in the sight of the world trying to fool people that you were at least once wise with your trickery. But today your bag of tricks have absolutely run out. The whole world can see what you're doing.

The press whips up hysteria in the white public. Then it shifts gears and starts working trying to get the sympathy of the white public. And then it shifts gears and gets the white public to support whatever criminal action they're getting ready to involve the United States in.

Remember how they referred to the hostages as "white hostages." Not "hostages." They said these "cannibals" in the Congo had "white hostages." Oh, and this got you all shook up. White nuns, white priests, white missionaries. What's the difference between a white hostage and a Black hostage? What's the difference between a white life and a Black life? You must think there's a difference, because your press specifies whiteness. "Nineteen white hostages" cause you to grieve in your heart. [*Laughter and applause*]

During the months when bombs were being dropped on Black people by the hundreds and the thousands, you said nothing. And you did nothing. But as soon as a few—a handful of white people who didn't have any business getting caught up in that thing in the first place—[*Laughter and applause*]—as soon as their lives became involved, you got concerned.

I was in Africa during the summer when they—when the mercenaries and the pilots were shooting down Black people in the Congo like flies. It wouldn't even get mentioned in the Western press. It wasn't mentioned. If it was mentioned, it was mentioned in the classified section of the newspaper. Someplace where you'd need a microscope to find it.

And at that time the African brothers, at first they weren't taking hostages. They only began to take hostages when they found that these pilots were bombing their villages. And then they took hostages, moved them into the village, and warned the pilots that if you drop bombs on the village, you'll hit your own people. It was a war maneuver. They were at war. They only held a hostage in a village to keep the mercenaries from murdering on a mass scale the people of those villages. They weren't keeping them as hostages because they were cannibals. Or because they thought their flesh was tasty. Some of those missionaries had been over there for forty years and didn't get eaten up. [*Laughter and applause*] If they were going to eat them they would have eaten them when they were young and tender. [*Laughter and applause*] Why you can't even digest that old white meat on an old chicken. [*Laughter*]

It's imagery. They use their ability to create images, and then they use these images that they've created to mislead the people. To confuse the people and make the people accept wrong as right and reject right as wrong. Make the people actually think that the criminal is the victim and the victim is the criminal.

Even as I point this out, you may say, "What does this all have to do with the Black man in America? And what does it have to do with the Black and white relations here in Rochester?"

You have to understand it. Until 1959 the image of the African continent was created by the enemies of Africa. Africa was a land dominated by outside powers. A land dominated by Europeans. And as these Europeans dominated the continent of Africa, it was they who created the image of Africa that was projected abroad. And they projected Africa and the people of Africa in a negative image, a hateful image. They made us think that Africa was a land of jungles, a land of animals, a land of cannibals and savages. It was a hateful image.

And because they were so successful in projecting this negative image of Africa, those of us here in the West of African ancestry, the Afro-American, we looked upon Africa as a hateful place. We looked upon the African as a hateful person. And if you referred to us as an African it was like putting us as a servant, or playing house, or talking about us in the way we didn't want to be talked.

Why? Because those who oppress know that you can't make a person hate the root without making them hate the tree. You can't hate your own and not end up hating yourself. And since we all originated in Africa, you can't make us hate Africa without making us hate ourselves. And they did this very skillfully.

And what was the result? They ended up with 22 million Black people here in America who hated everything about us that was African. We hated the African characteristics, the African characteristics. We hated our hair. We hated our nose, the shape of our nose, and the shape of our lips, the color of our skin. Yes we did. And it was you who taught us to hate ourselves simply by shrewdly maneuvering us into hating the land of our forefathers and the people on that continent.

As long as we hated those people, we hated ourselves. As long as we hated what we thought they looked like, we hated what we actually looked like. And you call me a hate teacher. Why, you taught us to hate ourselves. You taught the world to hate a whole race of people and have the audacity now to blame us for hating you simply because we don't like the rope that you put around our necks. [*Applause*]

When you teach a man to hate his lips, the lips that God gave him, the shape of the nose that God gave him, the texture of the hair that God gave him, the color of the skin that God gave him, you've committed the worst crime that a race of people can commit. And this is the crime that you've committed.

Our color became a chain, a psychological chain. Our blood—African blood—became a psychological chain, a prison, because we were ashamed of it. We believe—they would tell it to your face, and say they weren't; they were! We felt trapped because our skin was black. We felt trapped because we had African blood in our veins.

This is how you imprisoned us. Not just bringing us over here and making us slaves. But the image that you created of our motherland and the image that you created of our people on that continent was a trap, was a prison, was a chain, was the worst form of slavery that has ever been invented by a so-called civilized race and a civilized nation since the beginning of the world.

You still see the result of it among our people in this country today. Because we hated our African blood, we felt inadequate, we felt inferior, we felt helpless. And in our state of helplessness, we wouldn't work for ourselves. We turned to you for help, and then you wouldn't help us. We didn't feel adequate. We turned to you for advice and you gave us the wrong advice. Turned to you for direction and you kept us going in circles.

But a change has come about. In us. And what from? Back in '55 in Indonesia, at Bandung, they had a conference of dark-skinned people. The people of Africa and Asia came together for the first time in centuries. They had no nuclear weapons, they had no air fleets, no navy. But they discussed their plight and they found that there was one thing that all of us had in common—oppression, exploitation, suffering. And we had a common oppressor, a common exploiter.

If a brother came from Kenya and called his oppressor an Englishman; and another came from the Congo, he called his oppressor a Belgian; another came from

Guinea, he called his oppressor French. But when you brought the oppressors together there's one thing they all had in common, they were all from Europe. And this European was oppressing the people of Africa and Asia.

And since we could see that we had oppression in common and exploitation in common, sorrow and sadness and grief in common, our people began to get together and determined at the Bandung Conference that it was time for us to forget our differences. We had differences. Some were Buddhists, some were Hindus, some were Christians, some were Muslim, some didn't have any religion at all. Some were socialists, some were capitalists, some were communists, and some didn't have any economy at all. But with all of the differences that existed, they agreed on one thing, the spirit of Bandung was, from there on in, to de-emphasize the areas of difference and emphasize the areas that we had in common.

And it was the spirit of Bandung that fed the flames of nationalism and freedom not only in Asia, but especially on the African continent. From '55 to '60 the flames of nationalism, independence on the African continent, became so bright and so furious, they were able to burn and sting anything that got in its path. And that same spirit didn't stay on the African continent. It somehow or other—it slipped into the Western Hemisphere and got into the heart and the mind and the soul of the Black man in the Western Hemisphere who supposedly had been separate from the African continent for almost 400 years.

But the same desire for freedom that moved the Black man on the African continent began to burn in the heart and the mind and the soul of the Black man here, in South America, Central America, and North America, showing us we were not separated. Though there was an ocean between us, we were still moved by the same heartbeat.

The spirit of nationalism on the African continent—It began to collapse; the powers, the colonial powers, they couldn't stay there. The British got in trouble in Kenya, Nigeria, Tanganyika, Zanzibar, and other areas of the continent. The French got in trouble in the entire French Equatorial North Africa, including Algeria. Became a trouble spot for France. The Congo wouldn't any longer permit the Belgians to stay there. The entire African continent became explosive from '54-'55 on up to 1959. By 1959 they couldn't stay there any longer.

It wasn't that they wanted to go. It wasn't that all of a sudden they had become benevolent. It wasn't that all of a sudden they had ceased wanting to exploit the Black man of his natural resources. But it was the spirit of independence that was burning in the heart and mind of the Black man. He no longer would allow himself to be colonized, oppressed, and exploited. He was willing to lay down his life and take the lives of those who tried to take his, which was a new spirit.

The colonial powers didn't leave. But what did they do? Whenever a person is playing basketball, if—you watch him—the players on the opposing team trap him and he doesn't want to get rid of, to throw the ball away, he has to pass it to someone who's in the clear, who's on the same team as he. And since Belgium and France and Britain and these other colonial powers were trapped—they were exposed as colonial powers—they had to find someone who was still in the clear, and the only one in the clear so far as the Africans were concerned was the United States. So they passed the ball to the United States. And this administration picked it up and ran like mad ever since. [*Laughter and applause*]

As soon as they grabbed the ball, they realized that they were confronted with a new problem. The problem was that the Africans had awakened. And in their awakening they were no longer afraid. And because the Africans were not afraid, it was impossible for the European powers to stay on that continent by force. So our State Department, grabbing the ball and in their new analysis, they realized that they had to use a new strategy if they were going to replace the colonial powers of Europe.

What was their strategy? The friendly approach. Instead of coming over there with their teeth gritted, they started smiling at the Africans. "We're your friends." But in order to convince the African that he was their friend he had to start off pretending like they were our friend.

You didn't get the man to smile at you because you were bad, no. He was trying to impress your brother on the other side of the water. He smiled at you to make his smile consistent. He started using a friendly approach over there. A benevolent approach. A philanthropic approach. Call it benevolent colonialism. Philanthropic imperialism. Humanitarianism backed up by dollarism. Tokenism. This is the approach that they used. They didn't go over there well meaning. How could you leave here and go on the African continent with the Peace Corps and Cross Roads and these other outfits when you're hanging Black people in Mississippi? How could you do it? [*Applause*]

How could you train missionaries, supposedly over there to teach them about Christ, when you won't let a Black man in your Christ's church right here in Rochester, much less in the South. [*Applause*] You know that's something to think about. It gets me hot when I think about it. [*Laughter*]

From 1954 to 1964 can easily be looked upon as the era of the emerging African state. And as the African state emerged from '54 to '64, what impact, what effect did it have on the Afro-American, the Black American? As the Black man in Africa got independent, it put him in a position to be master of making his own image. Up until 1959 when you and I thought of an African, we thought of someone naked, coming with the tom-toms, with bones in his nose. Oh yeah!

This was the only image you had in your mind of an African. And from '59 on when they begin to come into the

UN and you'd see them on the television you'd get shocked. Here was an African who could speak better English than you. He made more sense than you. He had more freedom than you. Why places where you couldn't go—[*Applause*]—places where you couldn't go, all he had to do was throw on his robes and walk right past you. [*Laughter and applause*]

It had to shake you up. And it was only when you'd become shook up that you began to really wake up. [*Laughter*]

So as the African nations gained their independence and the image of the African continent began to change, the things agreed as the image of Africa switched from negative to positive. Subconsciously. The Black man throughout the Western Hemisphere, in his subconscious mind, began to identify with that emerging positive African image.

And when he saw the Black man on the African continent taking a stand, it made him become filled with the desire also to take a stand. The same image, the same—just as the African image was negative—and you hear about old hat in the hand, compromising, fearful looks—we were the same way. But when we began to read about Jomo Kenyatta and the Mau Mau and others, then you find Black people in this country began to think along the same line. And more closely along the same line than some of them really want to admit.

When they saw—just as they had to change their approach with the people on the African continent, they also then began to change their approach with our people on this continent. As they used tokenism and a whole lot of other friendly, benevolent, philanthropic approaches on the African continent, which were only token efforts, they began to do the same thing with us here in the States.

Tokenism. They came up with all kinds of programs that weren't really designed to solve anybody's problems. Every move they made was a token move. They never made a real down-to-earth move at one time to really solve the problem. They came up with a Supreme Court desegregation decision that they haven't put into practice yet. Not even in Rochester, much less in Mississippi. [*Applause*]

They fooled the people in Mississippi by trying to make it appear that they were going to integrate the University of Mississippi. They took one Negro to the university backed up with about 6,000—15,000 troops, I think it was. And I think it cost them $6 million. [*Laughter*]

And three or four people got killed in the act. And it was only an act. Now, mind you, after one of them got in, they said there's integration in Mississippi. [*Laughter*]

They stuck two of them in the school in Georgia and said there's integration in Georgia. Why you should be ashamed. Really, if I was white, I'd be so ashamed I'd crawl under a rug. [*Laughter and applause*] And I'd feel so low while I was under that rug I wouldn't even leave a hump. [*Laughter*]

This tokenism, this tokenism was a program that was designed to protect the benefits of only a handful of handpicked Negroes. And these handpicked Negroes were given big positions, and then they were used to open up their mouths to tell the world, "Look at how much progress we're making." He should say, look at how much progress he is making. For while these handpicked Negroes were eating high on the hog, rubbing elbows with white folk, sitting in Washington, D.C., the masses of Black people in this country continued to live in the slum and in the ghetto. The masses, [*Applause*] the masses of Black people in this country remain unemployed, and the masses of Black people in this country continue to go to the worst schools and get the worst education.

Along during the same time appeared a movement known as the Black Muslim movement. The Black Muslim movement did this: Up until the time the Black Muslim movement came on the scene, the NAACP was regarded as radical. [*Laughter*] They wanted to investigate it. They wanted to investigate it. CORE and all the rest of them were under suspect, under suspicion. King wasn't heard of. When the Black Muslim movement came along talking that kind of talk that they talked, the white man said, "Thank God for the NAACP." [*Laughter and applause*]

The Black Muslim movement has made the NAACP acceptable to white folks. It made its leaders acceptable. They then began to refer to them as responsible Negro leaders. [*Laughter*] Which meant they were responsible to white folk. [*Applause*] Now I am not attacking the NAACP. I'm just telling you about it. [*Laughter*] And what makes it so bad, you can't deny it. [*Laughter*]

So this is the contribution that that movement made. It frightened a lot of people. A lot of people who wouldn't act right out of love begin to act right out of fear. Because Roy [Wilkins] and [James] Farmer and some of the others used to tell white folk, look if you don't act right by us you're going to have to listen to them. They used us to better their own position, their own bargaining position. No matter what you think of the philosophy of the Black Muslim movement, when you analyze the part that it played in the struggle of Black people during the past twelve years you have to put it in its proper context and see it in its proper perspective.

The movement itself attracted the most militant, the most dissatisfied, the most uncompromising elements of the Black community. And also the youngest elements of the Black community. And as this movement grew, it attracted such a militant, uncompromising, dissatisfied element.

The movement itself was supposedly based upon the religion of Islam and therefore supposedly a religious movement. But because the world of Islam or the orthodox Muslim world would never accept the Black Muslim movement as a bona fide part of it, it put those of us who were in it in a sort of religious vacuum. It put us in a position of identifying ourselves by a religion, while the world in which that religion was practiced rejected us as not being bona fide practicers, practitioners of that religion.

Also the government tried to maneuver us and label us as political rather than religious so that they could charge us with sedition and subversion. This is the only reason. But although we were labeled political, because we were never permitted to take part in politics we were in a vacuum politically. We were in a religious vacuum. We were in a political vacuum. We were actually alienated, cut off from all type of activity with even the world that we were fighting against.

We became a sort of a religious-political hybrid, all to ourselves. Not involved in anything but just standing on the sidelines condemning everything. But in no position to correct anything because we couldn't take action.

Yet at the same time, the nature of the movement was such that it attracted the activists. Those who wanted action. Those who wanted to do something about the evils that confronted all Black people. We weren't particularly concerned with the religion of the Black man. Because whether he was a Methodist or a Baptist or an atheist or an agnostic, he caught the same hell.

So we could see that we had to have some action, and those of us who were activists became dissatisfied, disillusioned. And finally dissension set in and eventually a split. Those who split away were the real activists of the movement who were intelligent enough to want some kind of program that would enable us to fight for the rights of all Black people here in the Western Hemisphere.

But at the same time we wanted our religion. So when we left, the first thing we did we regrouped into a new organization known as the Muslim Mosque, headquartered in New York. And in that organization we adopted the real, orthodox religion of Islam, which is a religion of brotherhood. So that while accepting this religion and setting up an organization which could practice that religion—and immediately this particular Muslim Mosque was recognized and endorsed by the religious officials of the Muslim world.

We realized at the same time we had a problem in this society that went beyond religion. And it was for that reason we set up the Organization of Afro-American Unity in which anybody in the community could participate in an action program designed to bring about complete recognition and respect of Black people as human beings.

And the motto of the Organization of Afro-American Unity is By Any Means Necessary. We don't believe in fighting a battle that's going to—in which the ground rules are to be laid down by those who suppress us. We don't believe that we can win in a battle where the ground rules are laid down by those who exploit us. We don't believe that we can carry on a struggle trying to win the affection of those who for so long have oppressed and exploited us.

We believe that our fight is just. We believe that our grievances are just. We believe that the evil practices against Black people in this society are criminal and that those who engage in such criminal practices are to be looked upon themselves as nothing but criminals. And we believe that we are within our rights to fight those criminals by any means necessary.

This doesn't mean that we're for violence. But we do—we have seen that the federal government has shown its inability, its absolute unwillingness, to protect the lives and the property of Black people. We have seen where organized white racists, Klansmen, Citizens' Councilmen, and others can come into the Black community and take a Black man and make him disappear and nothing be done about it. We have seen that they can come in—[*Applause*]

We reanalyzed our condition. When we go back to 1939, Black people in America were shining shoes. Some of the most educated were shining in Michigan, where I came from, in Lansing, the capital. The best jobs you could get in the city were carrying trays out at the country club to feed white people. And usually the waiter at the country club was looked upon as the town big shot 'cause he had a good job around "good" white folks, you know. [*Laughter*]

He had the best education, but he'd be shining shoes right at the State House, the capitol. Shining the governor's shoes, and the attorney general's shoes, and this made him in the know, you know, 'cause he could shine white folks' shoes who were in big places. Whenever the people downtown wanted to know what was going on in the Black community, he was their boy. He was what's known as the "town Negro," the Negro leader. And those who weren't shining shoes, the preachers, also had a big voice in the community. That's all they'd let us do is shine shoes, wait on tables, and preach. [*Laughter*]

In 1939, before Hitler went on the rampage, or rather at the time—yeah, before Hitler went on the rampage, a Black man couldn't even work in the factory. We were digging ditches on WPA. Some of you all have forgotten too quick. We were ditchdigging on the WPA. Our food came from the welfare, they were stamped "not to be sold." I got so many things from the store called "not to be sold," I thought that was a store some place. [*Laughter*]

This is the condition the Black man was in, and that's till 1939. . . . Until the war started, we were confined to these menial tasks. When the war started, they wouldn't even take us in the army. A Black man wasn't drafted. Was he or was he not? No! You couldn't join the navy. Remember that? Wouldn't draft one. This was as late as 1939 in the United States of America!

They taught you to sing "sweet land of liberty" and the

rest of that stuff. No! You couldn't join the army. You couldn't join the navy. They wouldn't even draft you. They only took white folks. They didn't start drafting us until the Negro leader opened up his big mouth, [*Laughter*] talking about, "If white folks must die, we must die too." [*Laughter and applause*]

The Negro leader got a whole lot of Negroes killed in World War II who never had to die. So when America got into the war, immediately she was faced with a manpower shortage. Up until the time of the war, you couldn't get inside of a plant. I lived in Lansing, where Oldsmobile's factory was and Reo's. There was about three in the whole plant and each one of them had a broom. They had education. They had gone to school. I think one had gone to college. But he was a "broomologist." [*Laughter*]

When times got tough and there was a manpower shortage, then they let us in the factory. Not through any effort of our own. Not through any sudden moral awakening on their part. They needed us. They needed manpower. Any kind of manpower. And when they got desperate and in need, they opened up the factory door and let us in.

So we began to learn to run machines. Then we began to learn how to run machines, when they needed us. Put our women in as well as our men. As we learned to operate the machines, we began to make more money. As we began to make more money, we were able to live in a little better neighborhood. When we moved to a little better neighborhood, we went to a little better school. And when we went to that better school, we got a little better education and got in a little better position to get a little better job.

It was no change of heart on their part. It was no sudden awakening of their moral consciousness. It was Hitler. It was Tojo. It was Stalin. Yes, it was pressure from the outside, at the world level, that enabled you and me to make a few steps forward.

Why wouldn't they draft us and put us in the army in the first place? They had treated us so bad, they were afraid that if they put us in the army and give us a gun and showed us how to shoot it—[*Laughter*] they feared that they wouldn't have to tell us what to shoot at. [*Laughter and applause*]

And probably they wouldn't have had. It was their conscience. So I point this out to show that it was not change of heart on Uncle Sam's part that permitted some of us to go a few steps forward. It was world pressure. It was threat from outside. Danger from outside that made it—that occupied his mind and forced him to permit you and me to stand up a little taller. Not because he wanted us to stand up. Not because he wanted us to go forward. He was forced to.

And once you properly analyze the ingredients that opened the doors even to the degree that they were forced open, when you see what it was, you'll better understand your position today. And you'll better understand the strategy that you need today. Any kind of movement for freedom of Black people based solely within the confines of America is absolutely doomed to fail. [*Applause*]

As long as your problem is fought within the American context, all you can get as allies is fellow Americans. As long as you call it civil rights, it's a domestic problem within the jurisdiction of the United States government. And the United States government consists of segregationists, racists. Why the most powerful men in the government are racists. This government is controlled by thirty-six committees. Twenty congressional committees and sixteen senatorial committees. Thirteen of the twenty congressmen that make up the congressional committees are from the South. Ten of the sixteen senators that control the senatorial committees are from the South. Which means, that of the thirty-six committees that govern the foreign and domestic directions and temperament of the country in which we live, of the thirty-six, twenty-three of them are in the hands of racists. Outright, stone-cold, dead segregationists. This is what you and I are up against. We are in a society where the power is in the hands of those who are the worst breed of humanity.

Now how are we going to get around them? How are we going to get justice in a Congress that they control? Or a Senate that they control? Or a White House that they control? Or from a Supreme Court that they control?

Look at the pitiful decision that the Supreme Court handed down. Brother, look at it! Don't you know these men on the Supreme Court are masters of legal—not only of law, but legal phraseology. They are such masters of the legal language that they could very easily have handed down a desegregation decision on education so worded that no one could have gotten around. But they come up with that thing worded in such a way that here ten years have passed, and there's all kind of loopholes in it. They knew what they were doing. They pretend to give you something while knowing all the time you can't utilize it.

They come up last year with a civil rights bill that they publicized all around the world as if it would lead us into the promised land of integration. Oh yeah! Just last week, the Right Reverend Dr. Martin Luther King come out of the jail house and went to Washington, D.C., saying he's going to ask every day for new legislation to protect voting rights for Black people in Alabama. Why? You just had legislation. You just had a civil rights bill. You mean to tell me that that highly publicized civil rights bill doesn't even give the federal government enough power to protect Black people in Alabama who don't want to do anything but register? Why it's another foul trick, 'cause they . . . tricked us year in and year out. Another foul trick. [*Applause*]

So, since we see—I don't want you to think I'm teaching hate. I love everybody who loves me. [*Laughter*] But I sure don't love those who don't love me. [*Laughter*]

Since we see all of this subterfuge, this trickery, this maneuvering—it's not only at the federal level, the national level, the local level, all levels. The young generation of Blacks that's coming up now can see that as long as we wait for the Congress and the Senate and the Supreme Court and the president to solve our problems, you'll have us waiting on tables for another thousand years. And there aren't no days like those.

Since the civil rights bill—I used to see African diplomats at the UN crying out against the injustice that was being done to Black people in Mozambique, in Angola, the Congo, in South Africa, and I wondered why and how they could go back to their hotels and turn on the TV and see dogs biting Black people right down the block and policemen wrecking the stores of Black people with their clubs right down the block, and putting water hoses on Black people with pressure so high it tear our clothes off, right down the block. And I wondered how they could talk all that talk about what was happening in Angola and Mozambique and all the rest of it and see it happen right down the block and get up on the podium in the UN and not say anything about it.

But I went and discussed it with some of them. And they said that as long as the Black man in America calls his struggle a struggle of civil rights—that in the civil rights context, it's domestic and it remains within the jurisdiction of the United States. And if any of them open up their mouths to say anything about it, it's considered a violation of the laws and rules of protocol. And the difference with the other people was that they didn't call their grievances "civil rights" grievances, they called them "human rights" grievances. "Civil rights" are within the jurisdiction of the government where they are involved. But "human rights" is part of the charter of the United Nations.

All the nations that signed the charter of the UN came up with the Declaration of Human Rights and anyone who classifies his grievances under the label of "human rights" violations, those grievances can then be brought into the United Nations and be discussed by people all over the world. For as long as you call it "civil rights" your only allies can be the people in the next community, many of whom are responsible for your grievance. But when you call it "human rights" it becomes international. And then you can take your troubles to the World Court. You can take them before the world. And anybody anywhere on this earth can become your ally.

So one of the first steps that we became involved in, those of us who got into the Organization of Afro-American Unity, was to come up with a program that would make our grievances international and make the world see that our problem was no longer a Negro problem or an American problem but a human problem. A problem for humanity. And a problem which should be attacked by all elements of humanity. A problem that was so complex that it was impossible for Uncle Sam to solve it himself and therefore we want to get into a body or conference with people who are in such positions that they can help us get some kind of adjustment for this situation before it gets so explosive that no one can handle it.

Thank you. [*Applause*]

Index

Other titles from Pathfinder

THE STRUGGLE IS MY LIFE

"My political beliefs have been explained in my autobiography, *The Struggle Is My Life.*"—Nelson Mandela
by Nelson Mandela, $12.95

THE EASTERN AIRLINES STRIKE

Accomplishments of the Rank-and-File Machinists

The story of the 1990-91 strike against Eastern Airlines by members of the International Association of Machinists that prevented notorious union-buster Frank Lorenzo from turning Eastern into a profitable nonunion airline.

by Ernie Mailhot and others, $8.95

THE JEWISH QUESTION

A Marxist Interpretation

Explains the historical roots of anti-Semitism and how in times of social crisis it is used by the capitalists to mobilize reactionary forces against the labor movement and divide working people in face of their common exploiters.

by Abram Leon, $16.95

COSMETICS, FASHIONS, AND THE EXPLOITATION OF WOMEN

How big business uses women's second-class status to generate profits for a few and perpetuate the oppression of a sex and the exploitation of all working people.

by Joseph Hansen and Evelyn Reed with an introduction by Mary-Alice Waters, $11.95

CHANGING FACE OF U.S. POLITICS

The Proletarian Party and the Trade Unions

Building a revolutionary workers party in a world of capitalist economic crises, wars, trade conflicts, antiunion assaults, and attacks on workers' rights and individual liberties.

by Jack Barnes, $18.95

WRITE FOR A FREE CATALOG. SEE FRONT OF BOOK FOR ADDRESSES.

New International
A MAGAZINE OF MARXIST POLITICS AND THEORY

IN ISSUE 7

Opening Guns of World War III:
WASHINGTON'S ASSAULT ON IRAQ
BY JACK BARNES

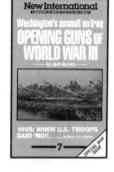

The U.S. government's murderous blockade, bombardment, and invasion of Iraq heralded a period of increasingly sharp conflicts among imperialist powers, more wars, and growing instability of the world capitalist system. $12.00

IN ISSUE 8

Che Guevara, Cuba, and the Road to Socialism

Exchanges from the early 1960s and today on the lasting importance and historical weight of the political and economic perspectives defended by Ernesto Che Guevara. $10.00

IN ISSUE 5

The Coming Revolution in South Africa

BY JACK BARNES

The world importance of the struggle to overthrow the apartheid system and the vanguard role of the African National Congress in leading the national, democratic revolution in South Africa to the end. $9.00

IN ISSUE 6

The Second Assassination of Maurice Bishop

BY STEVE CLARK

The accomplishments and lessons of the Grenada revolution under the leadership of Maurice Bishop, 1979-83. $10.00

DISTRIBUTED BY PATHFINDER

Further reading

TO SPEAK THE TRUTH
*Why Washington's 'Cold War'
against Cuba Doesn't End*

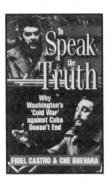

Fidel Castro and Che Guevara explain why the
U.S. government remains determined to destroy
the example set by the Cuban revolution and why
this effort will fail. With an introduction by
Mary-Alice Waters. 224 pp., $16.95

THE COMMUNIST MANIFESTO

Founding document of the modern revolutionary workers' movement,
written by Karl Marx and Frederick Engels. It explains how capitalism
works and charts the historic line of march of the world working class
toward the revolutionary struggle for socialism. 47 pp., $2.50

THE REVOLUTION BETRAYED
What Is the Soviet Union and Where Is It Going?

Leon Trotsky's classic study of the degeneration of the USSR explains the
roots of the crisis rocking the countries of the former Soviet bloc today.
314 pp., $18.95

HOW FAR WE SLAVES HAVE COME!
South Africa and Cuba in Today's World

Nelson Mandela and Fidel Castro, speaking together
in July 1991, discuss the antiapartheid struggle,
Cuba's contribution to it, and the unique role
played and example being set by the struggles of
the South African and Cuban peoples today.
83 pp., $7.95

Other books by and about Malcolm X

FEBRUARY 1965: THE FINAL SPEECHES

Speeches from the last three weeks of Malcolm X's life presenting the accelerating evolution of his political views. A large part is material previously unavailable, with some in print for the first time. $17.95

BY ANY MEANS NECESSARY

Speeches tracing the evolution of Malcolm's views on political alliances, intermarriage, women's rights, capitalism and socialism, and more. $15.95

MALCOLM X TALKS TO YOUNG PEOPLE

"The young generation of whites, Blacks, browns—you're living at a time of revolution." Speeches from Africa, Britain, and the United States. $9.95

MALCOLM X SPEAKS

"No, I'm not an American. I'm one of the 22 million black people who are victims of Americanism." Published in 1965, a classic selection. $16.95

MALCOLM X ON AFRO-AMERICAN HISTORY

Recounts the hidden history of the labor of people of African origin and their achievements—the better to prepare for the struggles of today. $7.95

HABLA MALCOLM X [MALCOLM X SPEAKS]

The best Spanish-language anthology of Malcolm X's speeches, interviews, and statements. $16.95

THE LAST YEAR OF MALCOLM X

The Evolution of a Revolutionary
by George Breitman $13.95

ORDER FROM PATHFINDER. SEE FRONT OF BOOK FOR ADDRESSES.